PRAYER: FAITH, FOCUS, AND WORDS

HOW PRAYER WORKS AND HOW TO PRAY WITH DEPTH AND AWARENESS

DMITRIY DORONKIN

Dmitriy Doronkin

Prayer: Faith, Focus, and Words

Published by the author under the Practical Spirituality imprint.

www.practicalspirituality.co

First edition, 2026

Originally published in Russian as *Молитва: вера, фокус и слово*.

This book is not a textbook on religion, theology, or psychotherapy. It reflects the author's personal perspective on the spiritual practice of prayer and does not claim to represent any specific denomination or religious teaching.

Some names mentioned in this book have been changed to protect privacy.

Contact the author: support@practicalspirituality.co

To my wife Elena, without whom I would never be the man I am today.

CONTENTS

PART II
Going Deeper Within

PART III

Practice

INTRODUCTION

WHY I'M WRITING ABOUT THIS

Prayer is perhaps the simplest, most accessible, and most natural way for a person to connect with the invisible reality that surrounds us. And I think it's precisely because of its simplicity that it's often underestimated. Sometimes it seems like, in order to make contact with the Divine, we need something complex, unusual—almost magical. But if you look closely, the truly powerful and truly necessary things in life are almost always simple: water, fire, breath, and prayer.

This text is devoted to exactly that—the art of conscious prayer.

I decided to write this book because I feel that many of us have somehow forgotten how to speak with God. Many people see prayer either as a strange ritual, or as an incomprehensible tongue-twister they were taught in childhood, or as a last resort in a difficult moment. But prayer is not simply the repetition of words. It is a special inner action that brings us into a different state of mind and heart. It is a living, natural way to stay in contact: with ourselves, with life, and with something much greater than we are.

I myself don't belong to any single spiritual or religious

tradition. My path is a search—an attempt to make sense of my own way through life, drawing on experience, knowledge, and insights. I have tried various spiritual practices, explored different religious traditions, and prayed in many different states. And one of the things that has remained and taken root in my life is prayer—not simply as a habit, but as a spiritual practice that sustains me: in difficult situations, in pain, in anxiety, in gratitude, in love.

This book is not a textbook, not a dogma, and not a collection of quotations. It is a reflection, an observation, an attempt to share what I myself have experienced, understood, and tested. I want to show that prayer can be a simple and useful tool for a living connection between the Divine Presence and us.

If what I've written here helps you on your life path, strengthens your inner support, and helps you feel a little more deeply that you are not alone, then my work and effort were not in vain.

What Prayer Is for Me

For me, prayer is a conversation that expresses my thoughts and emotions in a particular moment. Not a *"correct"* text, not a set of *"necessary"* words, but an ordinary, honest conversation with the One who is greater than I am. Sometimes it is spoken aloud, sometimes only inwardly. Sometimes it is several long sentences, and sometimes just one word or phrase: *"Help." "Thank you." "May the Lord bless you."*

Prayer is a connection that joins me with the Divine Presence. In joy, when words of gratitude pour out on their own. In sorrow, when my heart is breaking with pain. In difficult moments, when I stop pretending that I have everything under control and can say directly: *"I don't understand what to do next," "I don't know how to act," "I'm tired."* And at the same time, to know that I am being heard—even if I don't receive an answer *"from above"* right away.

And sometimes prayer is the beginning of silence in the soul. I sit, breathe, and inwardly say: *"Thank you for surrounding me with Your love and care."* And no eloquent words are needed anymore—only silence and grace.

It also happens that prayer is a short, emotional appeal in the middle of the day: on the road, in line, behind the wheel, at work. Gratitude for life, and a blessing for those who are nearby and help me move forward.

Put very simply, for me, prayer is a way not to lose connection: with myself, with people, with God. A way to remain attentive to my feelings and thoughts, and to meet any outward situation consciously.

What I Mean When I Say "God"

Before we go any further, I want to briefly clarify what I mean when I use the words *"God," "Lord," or "Divine Presence."*

For me, God is Spirit—present everywhere and in everything. God is not a *"person"* in the human sense, not a figure you can imagine as male or female. What I call God has no gender. For God, there is no difference between a man and a woman; your nationality, your sexual orientation, the color of your skin, or what you do or do not believe—none of it matters.

God is not an action, but a Presence. You could also put it this way: God is absolute Love. No matter who you are or what you have done in this life, God's love for you is unchanging. I believe in a Divine Presence that can support, guide, and inspire. What we call *"God's grace,"* I understand as moments when we feel this Presence especially clearly in our lives—sometimes through people, sometimes through events, and sometimes through the silence within ourselves.

At the same time, in this text, I will often use the word *"Lord"* and the pronoun *"He"* as is customary in the Russian religious tradition. Please don't take this as a claim that God is *"a man,"* or anything like that. It is simply a way of speaking. Behind these words, I always mean not a *"male figure in heaven,"* but a living, loving Divine Presence that is equally close to every person.

PART I

UNDERSTANDING PRAYER

1

WHAT PRAYER IS

Prayer is a conscious attempt to connect with the Divine through words, spoken aloud or silently in the mind.

To better understand what exactly happens during prayer and why it is capable of changing our inner and outer reality, let's break this *definition* down word by word. After all, it already contains the key meanings that determine how effective your prayer will become, and why sometimes it may seem that it "doesn't work" at all.

The first keyword is *"conscious."* This might seem obvious: *you can't* pray unconsciously. And that is indeed true. However, the level of our awareness at the moment we begin to pray directly influences the depth and strength of *that* prayer. Moreover, this largely determines the type of prayer we choose. I will speak about this in more detail *later*.

The next word is *"words."* Why are words spoken aloud so important? After all, there are many ways of connecting with the Divine—through meditation, ecstatic experiences, or even altered states of consciousness. But words have a unique power: they clarify intention, give an inner impulse a clear form, and help express what would otherwise remain unspoken. A word is a bridge between inner experience and outer expression—between what is in the heart and what is ready to *be expressed.* Words spoken aloud have a unique ability to change the space around us and to *directly influence* our immediate future.

The third keyword is *"attempt."* The mere fact that you pray does not mean that your prayer will necessarily be *"heard"*—and even *less* so, that you will receive the answer you want. Why this is so, and what it depends on, I will explain in the following chapters.

And finally, the main thing: *"to connect with the Divine."* In the Western tradition, the idea of one God is widespread, but unfortunately, many believers interpret it narrowly through the logic of exclusivity: the only *"true"* and *"right"* God is the God I believe in and the God I worship. In reality, the Divine—one in its essence—*can* manifest differently for each person. That is why it is so important to find your *own* perception of the Divine—the religious tradition, the spiritual path, the image that reflects your worldview and helps you deepen your spiritual connection with God as you experience Him.

2

THE INNER FORCES OF PRAYER

Because prayer is an integral part of religious and spiritual traditions, it makes sense to begin with what matters most: faith. This is where the dividing line between believers and atheists lies—between the conviction that the world and everything that happens in it is the result of chance and impersonal processes, and the understanding that behind this world —with its visible and invisible structure, its mathematics, its physics, its life—there is something greater.

I call this the Divine Presence, and I believe that everything that happens to us and around us has deep meaning.

From this arises the main question that every person who prays must answer: What do I believe in? What does God mean to me?

This is not a formal question—and by no means a simple one. As you search for an answer, an image of God gradually begins to emerge—the face of the Divine to whom you turn. The clearer this image, the deeper your awareness of your faith, and the stronger your connection with the One to whom you pray.

The Foundation of Prayer Is Faith

The power and effectiveness of prayer depend directly on your personal relationship with the Divine. That is why encountering the sacred elements of a tradition to which you do not inwardly belong—even if it enriches you culturally—often turns out to be spiritually *"deaf."* While an encounter with the sacred places of your own tradition can deeply strengthen your connection with the Divine toward which your soul strives.

The stronger this connection, the stronger the prayer. *"According to your faith, let it be done to you"* is not just words; it is one of the spiritual laws. It was true in the time of Christ and remains true to this day.

The Role of Doubt

Doubt is a natural part of the spiritual path. It often comes during periods of difficulty and spiritual searching, when the mind begins to ask: *"Will I be heard? Am I deceiving myself? Are my requests worthy?"*—and in doing so, it tests the strength of our faith. Such wavering does not in the least indicate *"weak"* faith; rather, it points to the soul's desire to deepen trust and connection with the Divine. Just as muscles grow stronger through tension and release, spiritual connection grows stronger as it passes through periods of confidence and doubt.

The main danger of doubt is not that it arises, but that it can split our inner state: a person speaks the words of prayer, yet inside remains tension and distrust; attention keeps slipping into anxious thoughts; a feeling arises that the prayer sounds formal, without deep emotional support. As a result, the effort of prayer weakens, and the prayer loses its strength and wholeness.

However, doubt can be turned from an obstacle into a tool for growth. When you notice it, don't push away or suppress your thoughts and emotions, but bring them into the light: speak your experience in the prayer itself, as in a trusting dialogue with the Divine. *"Lord, I have doubts—strengthen my faith"* is a simple but powerful formula that turns wavering into an act of sincerity.

Working with doubt often requires three steps. First, acknowledgment: honestly name the fears and questions that arise. Second, investigation: look for the causes of doubt—past disappointments, unmet expectations, limited ideas about God. Third, integration: return to the times when prayer has already borne fruit, and allow that experience to *"ground"* your mind. Gradually, doubt stops being an enemy: it becomes an entry point into a more mature trust, where faith rests not on denying questions, but on real answers verified by personal experience.

Strengthening Faith

Strengthening faith begins with regularly training your attention on the Divine Presence. One of the simplest but most powerful methods is a **prayer journal**. Write down everything you are grateful for, and every instance when you receive a response to your prayer: unexpected help, the right word, a feeling of inner calm in the middle of a storm. Over time, rereading these entries creates a chain of living confirmations: *"God has already been present and has helped me; my prayers have been heard—so I will receive an answer now as well."*

My friend Oksana kept such a journal, writing down even what seemed like small things: a free parking space, a timely call from an old friend. A year later, she reread her notebook and saw how a convincing picture of care took shape from these small *"coincidences."* Her prayer for a new job—one she had already stopped hoping for—was answered, after a dozen such little *"winks"* from life.

A second practice is **physical anchors of faith**. This might be a short prayer each time you light a candle, making the Sign of the Cross before leaving home, or the habit of taking three deep breaths and repeating the name of God when your heart is anxious. These gestures connect the spiritual with the everyday, helping you maintain inner awareness. Stability is born in rhythm: the same movement or the same word carries you into a space of trust, where doubt loses its power. A priest who served at a front-line hospital told me that before each surgery —when he accompanied the doctors and prayed for the wounded—he would take a small wooden cross in his hands, and the trembling would stop. That gesture connected him with all his past prayers and gave him courage.

Finally, faith grows **when it is shared.** Find a community—or at least one person—with whom you can discuss spiritual experiences without fear of criticism. Praying together, reading Scripture, and discussing questions leave less room for the inner *"voids"* where doubts usually take hold. In one of the home groups I led, we met once a week and shared where we had seen God's action. At first these were timid stories, but after a few months participants described deep changes: reconciliation in families, the healing of long-held resentments. The experience of others becomes a mirror in which you recognize your own path—and faith, reflected and multiplied, grows stronger.

Crisis of Faith

A crisis of faith is not a breakdown, but rather a *"reset"* of the spiritual system. Just as the body needs rest after hard work, the soul sometimes *"goes into the shadows"* in order to digest what it has accumulated.

The first step is **to allow yourself to be in this state without self-judgment.** Instead of your usual prayers, try the practice of silent presence: sit in silence, bring your attention to your breathing, and let the inner emptiness simply be. St. John of the Cross called such periods the *"dark night of the soul"*: not a time of punishment, but a space where a more mature, conscious faith ripens.

The second step is **a combination of a steady rhythm and concrete action.** Even if the words of prayer seem empty, keep the *"framework"* of your familiar practice: give yourself a minute of silence, take a few mindful breaths, write down one thing you're grateful for, and reread an inspiring line—from Scripture, poetry, or any wise book. And then translate the inner impulse into an outward act: support someone, do a kind deed, help where you can. Paradoxically, a tangible act of kindness often restores a sense of connection to something greater more quickly than attempts to *"squeeze"* a spiritual response from within.

The third step is **conversation and memory.** Find a spiritual mentor, or at least a trusted friend, with whom you can honestly share that *"it has been empty in the soul for a long time."* Voicing inner emptiness or emotional chaos is already halfway to healing. Then open an old prayer journal, letters, or photographs where the fruits of past prayers are visible. In moments of crisis, it is hard not simply to remember that things were once light; so let paper remind you. If there is no journal —create one right now, beginning with the acknowledgment: *"Today I feel emptiness."* Over time, this entry will become a point of reference from which you will see how a new, more conscious faith returns—gradually, not immediately, but much deeper and more lasting.

Focus as an Element of Prayer

When we direct our attention to something, we enter into a particular inner relationship with it. Focus is not merely observation—it is an act of inner connection between us and what we focus on. What we give our attention to begins to open more deeply—both in our perception and in how we experience reality. In this sense, prayer is a form of concentration: on God, on our connection with Him, on the Divine Presence.

We receive most of our information about the outside world through sight. That is why visual images—paintings, sculptures, icons—are so widely used in religious practice: they help direct attention, hold an inner state, and gather spiritual focus.

When we focus on a symbol or a sacred image, we begin to sense more clearly what lies beyond form—the Divine Presence to which prayer is addressed. That is its power—and also its limitation. An image is only a bridge from the outer to the inner, from form to essence. It is not the source of holiness; it points to it.

Images like a crucifix, icons of the Virgin Mary, and images of saints help us focus on the Divine. But at the same time, they can become an obstacle to further spiritual growth if a person begins to see the object itself—the icon, the statue, the image—as holy in itself, forgetting that it is only a tool, and not the Divine Presence itself.

The true power of prayer is revealed when the focus is not on an outer image, but on the inner experience of connection with the One to whom the words are addressed. It is focus that makes prayer alive, deep, and real—rather than a formal repetition of memorized phrases.

A short *"entry"* ritual can help you concentrate. Before prayer, find a quiet place, turn off your phone, sit comfortably, and take three slow breaths, silently repeating with each one: *"I am here—the Divine is with me."* Then put your intention into a single sentence—for example: *"I want to feel the Presence and ask for wisdom."* This simple action creates a clear inner *"frame"*: the mind understands that the next few minutes are devoted to connecting with the Divine, and distracting thoughts begin to lose their grip.

Visualization and Its Role in Prayer

Visualization is the deliberate use of imagination to deepen prayer and make it something you can feel inside. The brain responds to a vividly imagined image in much the same way it responds to a real experience; that is why an inner image can awaken a sense of closeness to the Divine no less than an external symbol.

Instead of simply saying the words, you begin to see what they mean: a warm light spreading from the heart, or your hand meeting an unseen hand. The image becomes a bridge. It turns the thought *"God is near"* into a concrete inner experience —one that is easier to hold your attention on.

Try a simple practice. Choose a focus for your attention. It can be an object: a candle, an icon, a cross, prayer beads, or a stone. Or it can be an inner image: the light of dawn, the smooth surface of water, a warm glow in your chest. Sit comfortably, close your eyes, take a few deep breaths, and bring the image to life with all your senses—not only how it looks, but how it sounds, feels, and even smells. If it is light, feel its warmth on your skin. If it is water, hear its gentle lapping.

Then pair your prayer with the image: as you inhale, let yourself fill with that sensation; as you exhale, speak a request or an expression of gratitude. When your mind wanders, return to the image without self-criticism. After a few minutes, you may feel the prayer moving through the image, rather than sounding like dry words.

The Power of Solitude

Another, deeper way to concentrate is prayer in solitude. In the Sermon on the Mount, Jesus says: *"When you pray, enter your inner room, shut your door, and pray to your Father who is in secret..."* (Matthew 6:6).

Our soul is always connected to God. But a restless mind—and the endless stream of outside information—can drown out that connection. Silence, solitude, quieting the mind, and personal prayer are among the most direct and effective ways to come into contact with the Divine.

For deep solitude, it helps to create a *"safety zone"*—a time and place where nothing requires an immediate response. Choose a place where you can be alone and know you won't be interrupted: your favorite chair, a bench in a quiet park, or even your car in a parking lot. What matters more than perfect silence is the feeling that here you won't have to explain yourself—to people or to your phone. Set an inner boundary: *"This is time only for inner dialogue."* Set a timer and turn the clock out of sight.

Before you begin praying, let your body become your ally. A couple of gentle stretches, a few deep breaths—and the tension that usually pulls your attention outward begins to soften. Keep one symbolic item nearby: a stone from the beach, a note of gratitude, a candle—not as a talisman, but as an anchor for your intention. Then close your eyes and allow silence to fill the space between your thoughts. The more clearly you feel that nothing external demands an answer from you right now, the easier it becomes to hear the soul's inner whisper—and the clearer and deeper your prayer becomes.

History shows us again and again: decisive breakthroughs often come in solitude. And this is not only a Christian intuition—many traditions have seen silence and solitude as a condition for deep spiritual experience. Moses climbed Mount Sinai and returned with a renewed understanding of the law—one that could unite an entire people. Silence became the soil for Siddhartha Gautama's insight, which we now call enlightenment. The Prophet Muhammad withdrew to the cave of Hira; there he received the first verses of the Qur'an, which would shape the lives of millions. And in the modern era, Henry

David Thoreau lived by Walden Pond to *"live deliberately"*; two years of voluntary solitude gave the world a book that still teaches us how to find freedom from social patterns.

What these stories share is not only physical distance from people, but an inner intention to listen all the way through the silence. Without the familiar background noise of other people's expectations, the deepest questions begin to rise: Who am I? What do I believe in? What do I live for? And when an answer ripens, a person returns to the world—now carrying a new word, a new law, a new idea—sometimes something that changes not only their own life, but the fate of whole cultures.

The Power of Words

The final essential element of prayer is the word. In everyday life, we often underestimate the power of what we say, without thinking about the influence our words have—both on ourselves and on the world around us.

I will devote a separate chapter to this topic, but even here it is important to say: the structure of prayer—its beginning, its main part, and its conclusion—shapes not only its inner rhythm, but also its strength. Every word spoken with intention and awareness fills prayer with depth and makes it living, directed, and real.

3

TYPES OF PRAYER

There are three main types of prayer: *petitionary, thanksgiving, and affirming*. Each reflects an inner worldview and a person's relationship to the Divine. The type of prayer we choose reveals how we see God—where God is in relation to us, what role God plays in our lives, and how connected we feel to Him.

Other common forms—praise, confession, blessing, and others—I see not as separate kinds of prayer, but as modes and elements that can be present within any of these three basic types.

Petitionary Prayer

This is the most common—and perhaps the oldest—type of prayer. As I sometimes joke, *"Who needs God when everything is going well?"*

A prayer of petition is an appeal to the Divine for help, protection, healing, or a way through a difficult situation. In it, a person acknowledges their limitations and opens their heart in hope of an answer from above.

The inner logic behind this kind of prayer often sounds like this: I am here, on earth, and I have problems. God is somewhere *"out there,"* far away, in His own world. God is almighty, but I'm not always sure I'm being heard—or whether I'm even worthy of His help. I turn to Him, hoping my prayer will be heard and that He will support me in what I cannot solve on my own.

It's important to understand that in different spiritual traditions, this kind of prayer can carry different meanings. Often a request is not a sign of despair, but a form of ongoing dialogue with the Divine—an expression of humility and hope, a recognition of our dependence on a higher will, and a plea for protection and mercy.

A prayer of petition is the voice of a heart that is not afraid to be heard.

A classic example is the Lord's Prayer, which Jesus gave to His disciples as a model. It is structured largely as petition: *"hallowed be...," "your kingdom come...," "your will be done...," "give us...," "forgive...," "deliver us...."* I will look at this prayer in detail in a later chapter.

Thanksgiving Prayer

At the heart of this kind of prayer is the sense that God is near. He is already present in a person's life: helping, supporting, giving signs, answering prayers. A natural feeling of gratitude arises in response.

Often, different tones are woven together within a single prayer—both petition and thanksgiving. We can give thanks for what we have already received and, at the same time, ask for something more. At the level of one's inner worldview, it is often experienced like this: God is greater than my understanding and beyond me, yet He hears and responds; I am grateful to Him for this—and I ask that His support continue.

Such prayers can be general:

"Thank You for everything that is already in my life. I feel Your presence. I trust You. I am grateful to You."

Or they can be more specific:

"Thank You that I wake up in the morning, for those who are close to me, and that You are guiding me—even when I don't notice it."

After Thanksgiving, it can be natural to move into an affirming prayer: not a request, but an inner *"yes"* to what we hold to be true.

Affirming Prayer

This type of prayer has become widespread over the last 100–120 years. It is based on a different perception of reality: God is not somewhere far away *"out there."* He is within me and around me—in every breath, in every moment. I am not God, but my soul is inseparably connected with Him: I am in Him, and He is in me.

From this perspective, God is experienced as love, life, clarity, peace, and strength. If difficulties arise in my life—for example, illness—there is, in this view, no need to beg for healing as if the connection with the Divine had been lost. The Divine already *"knows"* me, my problems, and my needs. The point is not to persuade God or earn His attention, but to affirm my inner agreement with this connection and to return to a sense of wholeness when it has been disturbed.

From this perspective, any problem can reflect a loss of inner wholeness—a temporary disruption in our connection to the Divine. Affirming prayer is a way to remember who we are and to restore that connection.

Here is an example of such a prayer:

"I am in You, and You are in me. You are the source of life, peace, and strength. Your fullness lives in me. I accept this as truth. I return to harmony. My body remembers wholeness, and I allow this knowing to surface. I choose light, peace, and health. I open myself to Your love. Let it be so."

~

ANY OF THESE THREE FORMS OF PRAYER CAN BE EFFECTIVE. IT depends not on *"correct"* wording, but on inner sincerity, faith, and a willingness to remain in contact with what you believe in.

On my spiritual path, I have used all three kinds of prayer. I know what it is like to ask from a place of desperation. I learned to give thanks even when I couldn't feel a response. And I practiced affirming prayer as a form of inner spiritual awakening and growth.

Today, I most often use thanksgiving prayer—not because it is *"better,"* but because that is where I feel closeness, trust, and peace. And yet I know that each of us has our own path, and the Divine hears us in any form as long as we speak from the heart.

For prayer to be conscious and effective, it matters not only which type you choose (petitionary, thanksgiving, or affirming), but also its modality—that is, its emotional tone and inner direction: praise, petition, thanksgiving, confession, blessing, trust, and silent listening. In the practical part of this book, we will return to this topic and look at how to combine modalities with the three basic types of prayer.

4

THE STRUCTURE OF A CLASSIC PRAYER

From a practical standpoint, I think it can be very helpful to look at how classic prayers are structured—in our case, within the Judeo-Christian tradition. And for that, the most common and instantly recognizable prayer—the Lord's Prayer —will serve us well.

The Lord's Prayer (Matthew 6:9–13, WEB)

"Our Father in heaven,
may your name be kept holy.
Let your Kingdom come.
Let your will be done on earth
as it is in heaven.
Give us today our daily bread.
Forgive us our debts,
as we also forgive our debtors.
Bring us not into temptation,
but deliver us from the evil one.
For yours is the Kingdom,

the power, and the glory forever.
Amen."

This prayer is one of the best-known examples of petitionary prayer, and its structure clearly reflects five key elements: the name of the Deity, His location, the relationship between the one praying and God, the petitions, and the closing.

Name of the Deity

When we address someone, we use their name or title.

Likewise, in classical prayer—across major religious and spiritual traditions—everything begins with an address: with speaking God's name.

Sometimes the form of this address also reveals how the person praying sees God—through masculine or feminine language, or through a deliberate rejection of gendered categories. We will talk about this a little later.

In the Lord's Prayer, the invocation is *"Our Father."* Christianity emerged from Judaism, and these words directly reflect that lineage.

The word *"Father"* frames God in paternal terms—meaning that in this prayer God is spoken of in masculine language. This is stated immediately and quite directly.

You may ask, *"So what, Dmitry?"* And I will answer: it is more important than it might seem at first glance. In different cultures and traditions, the Divine can be experienced as a feminine principle, as something beyond gender, or as a unity of both principles—it all depends on a person's worldview, faith, and inner image of God.

For example, in my spiritual community, some people begin their prayers with the words: *"Beloved Mother-Father God."* In English, this can sound a bit awkward. But the meaning is clear: it is an attempt to emphasize the dual nature of the Divine—the masculine and feminine principles in one.

In Islamic tradition, the name used for God is *"Allah,"* and the name itself does not specify gender. It is a name filled with meaning and holiness, yet not tied to gender categories.

The word *"our"* is also important. Judaism has long emphasized covenant—a special bond between God and a particular people. Alongside the proclamation of Divine unity, this language of belonging can gradually harden into the idea: *"God is one—and He is ours."* In its strongest form, it can sound like: only our God is true. Similar exclusivist notes later appear in Christianity, and then in Islam.

So the first element is the invocation: naming the One you are addressing. This is where it all begins.

The Location of God

The next element of a classic prayer is stating where the One we are addressing is. In the Lord's Prayer, the words are: *"in heaven."* This is the second key part—because it answers the question: Where is God in relation to us? And, as with everything else in prayer, it reflects the inner picture of reality held by the person praying.

In this case, God is in heaven, and human beings are on earth. After the address, the participants in the scene are placed: where He is and where we are. It creates a kind of spiritual *"geography"* that helps shape an inner picture of prayer.

I want to emphasize: this is not a formality. It is one of the most meaningful moments in prayer, because it is here that we quietly define where we stand—and how we sense the Presence of the One to whom we are speaking.

I remember attending a spiritual conference a few years ago. Before it began, a tall, beautiful, dark-skinned woman walked onto the stage. She approached the microphone and said in a deep, resonant voice: *"God is here. God is now."* Even now, when I remember it, I still get chills. Those words didn't just sound good—they expressed the worldview of everyone present. For them, God was not "out there," but here—among them, and within each of them. Right now.

The Qualities of God and the Relationship Between God and the One Who Prays

"May your name be kept holy. May your Kingdom come. May your will be done on earth as it is in heaven."

The third part of the prayer names God's qualities and shapes the relationship between the one who prays and God. In this example, it is an active recognition of God's holiness, power, and will in the world. Here, the person assents, calls, and opens themselves to the divine order.

"May your name be kept holy" is an acknowledgment of God's holiness. *"May your Kingdom come"* is a call for the coming of God's Kingdom. *"May your will be done on earth as it is in heaven"* is one of the most profound lines: an agreement that it is not my will, but His, that guides me.

Usually, in a classically structured prayer, after the address and the naming of *"where God is,"* there follows a movement of praise or an enumeration of divine qualities. This helps the person praying consciously shape their relationship with the Divine, expressing respect, recognition, and trust.

The Lord's Prayer serves as an example here, but the structure itself is found in many religious and spiritual traditions.

Petition

In most languages, we use the same verbs for requests and demands. In our example, these are the words: *"give," "forgive," "bring us not,"* and *"deliver us."* I often encounter prayers that sound like a long list of requests—and sometimes almost demands directed at the Divine.

But in the prayer we are looking at, before the petitions, there is an important line: *"Let your will be done on earth as it is in heaven."* It sets the inner tone. It reminds us that, despite all our desires, we bow to the Divine will. As a result, everything that follows sounds like a request rather than a command.

Now that the name has been spoken, the place has been named, and the relationship has been established, the moment of petition arrives:

"Give us today our daily bread.
Forgive us our debts,
as we also forgive our debtors.
Bring us not into temptation,
but deliver us from the evil one."

This part includes both material and spiritual needs: food, forgiveness, and protection. Interestingly, the requests are expressed in a general form—they are universal and do not refer to specific situations. In personal prayer, however, specificity often adds sincerity and deepens the prayer.

Conclusion

"For yours is the Kingdom,
the power, and the glory forever.
Amen."

Any good speech needs a fitting ending. Here, after all that has been said, divine power, glory, and eternity are affirmed once again.

In Christianity, as in Judaism and many other religious and spiritual traditions, prayer ends with the word *"Amen"*—a word that expresses agreement, trust, and confirmation of what has been spoken. Sometimes (in esoteric traditions), people draw a symbolic parallel with the sound *"Om"*—a sacred vibration that, in some traditions, is associated with the beginning of the universe.

As you can see, the structure of the Lord's Prayer is not accidental. Each part serves its own purpose—from establishing contact to forming a request and bringing the prayer to a close. It is not just a text, but a spoken spiritual form—a kind of rhythm of connection with the Divine.

Understanding this structure not only deepens your understanding of traditional prayers but also helps you shape your own prayers more consciously, more sincerely, and with more life.

I have intentionally focused only on the main types of prayer and the structure of classical prayer to give the narrative clarity and inner order. In reality, there is a wide variety of prayer practices in the world—from the shortest to the longest, from the strictly structured to the almost spontaneous.

For example, in Orthodox Christianity, there is a prayer consisting of just a few words: "*Lord, save and protect*"—simple and powerful.

In Hinduism, the sound *"Om"* is repeated as a sacred formula and used as a practice of concentration.

In Islam, the word *"Bismillah"* is often spoken before an action, both as an invocation and a blessing.

And on the other end of the spectrum, there are long, almost unstructured prayers in which what matters is not order, but spirit. One example is a Russian Orthodox prayer often attributed to the Optina elders—sincere, free, and rooted more in feeling than in form.

5

THE POWER OF WORDS AND EMOTIONS IN PRAYER

In this chapter, I want to take a closer look at two aspects of prayer that I consider key: the words we choose and the emotions that accompany them. But before we talk about the power of words, I want to make a short detour and touch on human energy capacity (in other words, our inner resources) and the principle of energy exchange.

Energy Capacity and the Principle of Energy Exchange

Each of us has a certain energy capacity—an inner reserve that includes our strength, desires, abilities, and material resources. This capacity shows itself on three levels: physical, emotional, and intellectual. It is reflected in the outer world as well: in how many responsibilities we take on, how many things we accumulate, how many relationships we maintain, and how well we cope with all of it.

Our inner system is constantly seeking balance between what is happening inside us and how our outer life is arranged. And every time we receive something, we inevitably give something in return. This principle of energy exchange shows up in many areas of life.

Want to be in better physical shape? You will have to give something: time, effort, and perhaps money—for exercise, discipline, and lifestyle changes.

Want to earn more? You need to invest intellectual energy in learning, development, and practice—and then share what you've gained with others through a product, a service, or results. Money, in this view, is also a form of energy—returned to you for what you have given.

You can't receive without giving. And this applies not only to the outer world, but to the inner one as well. We exchange energy through attention, words, emotions, and decisions. Prayer is no exception: it is also an act of exchange between us and the Divine Presence—one in which we invest attention, sincerity, and an inner willingness to remain in contact.

And this is where words come into play.

The Power of Words

"And what do words have to do with it?" you may ask.

The point is that many of us underestimate the power of words—and how they shape our inner state and the space around us. To make this clearer, let me offer a simple example. The very same event can leave a completely different inner imprint, depending on the words that accompany it.

Imagine this: someone close to you is late, or lets you down when it matters. The fact is the same. But from there, two different realities are possible.

In the first, you say: *"You're always like this. I can't rely on you."* In that moment, you're not simply describing the situation—you're passing judgment, and you create a rupture in the relationship. The other person gets defensive, shame or anger flares, and the conversation quickly turns into conflict. Trust—

and the relationship itself—becomes much harder to rebuild afterward.

In the second, you speak differently: *"This mattered to me. I'm upset that it turned out this way. What happened?"* These words don't change the facts, but they change the space between you: they open the possibility of a conversation without blame. Instead of a label, there is dialogue. Instead of escalation, there is a chance to understand, to acknowledge, to repair. And the connection between two people doesn't snap.

Someone might say: *"They're just words! What matters is the intention."* Yes—words are born from an inner decision. But they are also the way in which the decision takes form. If a word is sincere, if it is filled with meaning, it carries power—and that power changes the space between people.

Our words affect other people, animals, plants—and, in my experience, even objects. (Yes, even objects.)

Words are among the most important tools for changing both our inner and outer worlds. That is why, in prayer, the words we choose matter so much: prayer is an act of connection, in which every word becomes a thread linking us to the Divine Presence.

The Power of the Word in Spiritual Traditions

Many spiritual cultures begin their creation story with a word. In the Judeo-Christian Bible, we hear, *"Let there be light,"* and the world responds. In the prologue of the Gospel of John, we read, "In the beginning was the Word." In the Qur'an, the world comes into being through the divine word *"Kun!"*—*"Be!"*—and becomes reality. Ancient Indian traditions preserve the sound "Om" as the primal vibration upon which the cosmos rests. Different languages, different images—yet one shared intuition: the word does not merely describe reality; it helps shape it.

A similar principle operates on the human level as well. Buddhists place *"right speech"* on the Noble Eightfold Path as a condition of liberation; Sufis practice dhikr—the rhythmic remembrance of God; and many traditions hold that a spoken word, in a sense, releases a thought into the world and turns it into a force.

That is why, when we speak a prayer or an affirmation, we enter an ancient and universal stream. A reverent approach to words—precision of phrasing, a sincere emotional charge, and mindful silence between phrases—brings us closer to that same creative power that sages have spoken of for centuries. The word remains one of the most accessible—and, at the same time, one of the most powerful—tools of spiritual work.

Emotions as the Energy of Prayer

Words matter in prayer, but the *"engine"* of prayer is our emotional tone. When we are inwardly open and centered, prayer becomes clearer and stronger; when we are torn by fear and irritation, the sense of connection feels weaker.

Emotions aren't just reactions to external events; they are the state of the soul in a given moment, reflecting our inner world, shaped by our beliefs and thoughts.

Figuratively speaking, each emotion *"sounds"* in its own way —it's the music of the soul, with its own tones and degrees of inner tension. Joy, gratitude, and inspiration expand our perception and make it easier to feel close to the Divine. Fear, anger, irritation, and despair constrict our inner space and disrupt the natural flow of life.

Our emotional state influences the kind of prayer we speak and largely determines its power.

When we pray with trust and gratitude, we attune ourselves

to the state in which the Divine Presence is most readily felt. Conversely, a prayer spoken in anger, fear, or despair may feel unanswered—not because God *"does not hear"* us, but because we ourselves are closed off, tense, and inwardly divided in that moment.

You can think of it like tuning a radio: the transmitting and receiving sides have to be on the same frequency.

Imagine two prayers. The first is spoken with despair, fear, and disbelief:

"Lord, why is everything so bad? Why doesn't anyone help me? Where are You?"

The second is spoken with trust, gratitude, and inner openness:

"Lord, I don't understand everything, but I know You are near. Show me the way. Help me stay calm and steadfast until everything becomes clear."

In both cases, it is a request. But the emotional message is entirely different. The first prayer sounds like an alarm—full of static. The second is a clearer call for connection.

That is why it is important to remember: the power of prayer is revealed not only in its words, but also in how deeply those words reflect your inner state. Words carry meaning, but feelings give them force.

When words and feelings are in unison, true prayer is born—one that does not simply vanish into emptiness, but finds a path in both directions: toward the Divine, and back to us.

6

WHY AND WHEN PRAYERS DON'T WORK

We know—or at least have heard—stories of prayer that seem to truly help. Someone recovers despite the diagnosis. Someone suddenly receives long-awaited help. In a difficult moment, someone feels as if they are being supported and guided from within. I've always been drawn to stories like these. They don't just give us hope—they also make us pause and ask: is it really true, or is it simply a matter of happy coincidences?

But then why, in other situations—despite sincere requests, tears, and faith—does nothing happen? Why in one case does prayer become a living bridge between the one who prays and the Divine Presence, while in another it seems to vanish into emptiness?

In this chapter, I don't offer universal answers. I'm simply sharing observations and reflections that may help you understand the nature of prayer more clearly—and why it doesn't always yield the results we hope for. In my view, there can be several reasons.

Lack of Faith and a Weak Inner Connection

One of the first things that can keep prayer from bearing fruit is a lack of faith. Often, it points to a weak inner connection between the person praying and the Divine Presence to whom the prayer is addressed.

"According to your faith, be it done to you," Jesus says in the Gospel of Matthew (Matthew 9:29, WEB). These words underscore that faith is not an abstract concept, but a living state of the soul—one that makes a living connection with the Divine possible.

It isn't enough simply to begin praying—and genuinely expect an answer. What's needed is inner engagement: intellectual, emotional, and spiritual. You need a real connection with the image of God you believe in, and with the language of prayer you choose.

Unfortunately, many people treat prayer as a *"just in case"* measure. They remember it only in difficult times, come to church when they *"need something,"* and approach God with an unspoken expectation of exchange: *"I'll do my part—and You do Yours."*

I have often seen people rush into church late for a service, leave notes with prayer requests in passing, and then leave just as quickly—without even staying to the end.

This kind of behavior reflects a formal approach. It suggests neither inner depth nor a genuine connection with the Divine. And this is one reason prayer may seem to go unanswered.

Attachment to the Outcome

When we cling too tightly to a desired outcome, we begin to spend our energy on control. Prayer stops being an act of trust and turns into inner pressure:

"Do what I want. Look—I'm asking, I believe, I deserve it—so why isn't it happening?"

In this inner posture, there is too much control and too little space for miracles.

But the Divine is not a mechanism for fulfilling desires, nor a servant who must obey our ideas of what is right. The Divine is a living Presence—One we can enter into dialogue with, not One we issue ultimatums to. True prayer is not *"do this,"* but *"be with me."* Not *"give me this,"* but *"help me align with what is meant to unfold."*

The essence lies in maintaining a clear intention while letting go of control. In practice, it can sound like an inner formula:

"May the highest good be done—for me and for everyone involved."

We keep the goal in view, but we allow life to bring it about in the wisest way for everyone involved—even if the path turns out differently than we imagined.

Not Ready to Receive What You Ask For

Another obstacle that can stand in the way of an answered prayer is simply not being ready to receive what you're asking for.

Prayer is not a magic wand that instantly changes you or your circumstances. It is a way of attunement—of restoring inner harmony and clarifying your intention, one of the ways we connect with the Divine. It can open the way, but it won't take the steps for you.

If you ask for change but are not internally ready for it, your prayer may seem unanswered. Sometimes this shows up as doubt, fear of the new, or an unwillingness to let go of an old way of life that—while uncomfortable—still feels familiar.

For something to truly enter your life, it is not enough to want it. You must also be ready to receive it—to make room for it both within yourself and in your outer life.

The pause between prayer and its fulfillment is sometimes time given for inner preparation: time to mature, to overcome resistance, and to reach a new level of awareness.

What You Ask For May Not Be What You Need

Perhaps you don't truly need what you are praying for.

Yes, this may sound strange. But life shows us again and again that many of the things we once passionately wanted were not actually necessary for us—and, in a deeper sense, never were. I have seen this in my own life many times. Often, looking back, we say:

"Thank You, Lord, that it didn't happen... But I wanted it so much back then."

The Divine Presence, which cares for us far more than we realize, sometimes keeps certain things from entering our lives —things that could harm us or pull us away from what we truly need. In doing so, it protects us, even when it feels like rejection in the moment.

Being Open to an Unexpected Answer

Sometimes prayer does not bring a direct answer—but that does not mean there is no answer. It does not always come in words, actions, or obvious changes.

Sometimes the answer is a sudden inner calm, a stillness in

the heart. Sometimes it is simply that things don't get worse: everything could have fallen apart, but it doesn't. Sometimes it is an unexpected surge of strength that gets you through what once seemed unbearable. Sometimes it is a person who shows up at exactly the moment you need them.

The answer may not come as a change in external circumstances, but as a change in you—your state, your attitude, your inner outlook.

We wait for intervention, but receive support from a different direction. We wait for a miracle, but clarity comes instead. We wait for a *"yes,"* but what comes is a different kind of message: *"I am with you."* And in that, too, there is an answer —silent, gentle, but real.

Prayer is not always a way to change the world. Sometimes it is a way to avoid losing ourselves in what is happening to us.

Even if it seems your prayer has gone unanswered, don't rush to conclusions. Sometimes the result comes later. Sometimes it comes in a different form. Sometimes it comes as a quiet knowing that becomes clearer with time.

Prayer is always a movement: inward and toward the Divine. And if it was sincere, alive, real—it has already changed something in you. That means it has already begun to work.

PART II

GOING DEEPER WITHIN

7

PRAYER AND MEDITATION

Prayer and meditation are different but surprisingly complementary forms of communion with the Divine Presence.

In prayer, we express our feelings and emotions: we turn to the One who is greater than we are, open our hearts, ask, give thanks, and acknowledge what is true.

In meditation, we consciously slow down, let go of the flow of thought, and allow awareness to enter a space of inner silence—deep and peaceful—where one thought has ended, and the next has not yet begun.

The difference between them is not only in form, but also in the direction of attention. Prayer is directed toward the Divine: it seeks a response, a blessing, a connection. Meditation is directed inward: it creates a silence in which that response can be heard. Prayer is an act of turning; meditation is an act of presence. And yet both lead to the same place: connection with the Source, a return to the inner ground where there is more peace and truth.

One of the most beautiful bridges between them is guided meditation. A gentle voice guides a person through an inner process: it calms, directs attention, and helps them find support through breathing, images, and words. In this practice, you are not left alone with a restless mind—you are given structure, direction, and pace. Sometimes guided meditations include elements of prayer—phrases filled with faith, love, and longing. At that point, it becomes more than a relaxation technique: an inner journey in which words serve as a conduit to the sacred.

This format is especially valuable for those who find it difficult to enter silence, who don't know where to begin, or who have lost the feel for living prayer. In it, you can hear what was previously drowned out: fear, the desire to be loved, your need, and your gratitude. Sometimes such meditations restore a taste for sincere prayer, and sometimes they themselves become prayer—not spoken aloud, but lived from within.

Prayer and meditation are not opposites. They are two wings of the same inner work. One says, *"I am here. I want to be closer."* The other responds, *"Be. And just listen."* And when both wings move in harmony, true spiritual flight begins—simple, quiet, and deeply personal.

8

PRAYER AND KARMA

Karma is one of the most challenging—and at the same time, one of the fairest—ideas in spiritual life. It is not a punishment, a verdict, or a scare tactic. It is one of the spiritual laws: what we radiate will, sooner or later, return to us. Our actions, thoughts, words, and intentions leave a trace. Karma is like the universe's energetic memory. It does not condemn, seek revenge, or forget; it reflects, returns, and teaches.

Sometimes we encounter difficulties that seem undeserved. But if we look deeper—not through the lens of guilt, but through the lens of responsibility—we gradually begin to see that what is happening has a root cause. Even if that root lies in a past we no longer remember, it can still be at work—like a seed that eventually bears fruit.

And here a crucial question arises: can prayer change karma?

Prayer Does Not Cancel Karma—It Changes Us

Prayer does not erase consequences like a *"delete"* button. But it can transform something even more important: our inner state —and with it, the direction in which our life unfolds.

Prayer changes a person. And if you have begun praying regularly, you are no longer the same person who created the cause. If you change, the consequences may also take a different form.

Prayer is a way to step out of autopilot. You stop being merely a participant in events and become a co-creator of your destiny. Sometimes this is a gentle inner shift: more patience, more awareness, more acceptance. And sometimes it is a turning point after which what has been accumulating begins to be cleansed.

One of the most powerful moments in prayer is when it stops being a request and becomes an acknowledgment. When you speak the words not simply because you want to escape the consequences, but because you see, you understand, and you are ready to change. In that moment, a new level of relationship with karma begins: self-awareness.

Awareness is the courage to see how you created suffering —your own or someone else's—and to say: *"Yes, it happened. I see it. I don't want to live that way anymore. I have the chance to choose differently."* In that inner turn, spiritual alchemy is born. Recognition, repentance, and a willingness to change soften the karmic imprint—and sometimes transform it completely.

When "Things Get Worse"

We are used to thinking of prayer as a request for help. Yet often the *"answer"* is not relief, but the opposite: an intensification. What has been building for a long time rises to the surface. What was postponed becomes urgent. Sometimes it feels like things have only gotten worse—but often this is not deterioration. It is the beginning of real work.

Karma stops sitting in the background and moves to the foreground so that you can finally see it and work through it consciously. Sometimes what we fear most is what sets us free. Prayer does not always bring immediate relief; more often, it leads to purification—a process that is not always pleasant but can lead to a new beginning.

How to Pray While Moving Through Karmic Lessons

If you feel you are going through something karmic, don't ask for relief right away. Ask for understanding. Ask for strength. Ask for inner growth.

Here are a few phrases you can use in prayer:

"Show me what I'm meant to learn."
"Help me go through this with dignity." "
Cleanse my heart of resistance."
"Thank You that even this can serve my good."

Don't be afraid to be honest with God. And don't be afraid to be vulnerable. Prayer is the one place where you can be real —even if your *"real"* right now is tears, doubt, and pain. It is in that state that prayer comes alive—and karma becomes more workable, more responsive to change.

The meaning of prayer in the context of karma is not to *"escape punishment,"* but to walk through what has come and rise into higher states of consciousness. Not out of fear, but out of love. Not with the question *"Why?"* but with the question *"What for?"*

Karma is the consequence of the past. Prayer is an opportunity to understand the present and shape the future. By living in the present and praying, we can become different. And then even old causes begin to lead to new results.

9

PRAYER AS A PATH OF PERSONAL TRANSFORMATION

Prayer is not only a way to turn toward the Divine. It is also a way to speak honestly about what you truly feel. In genuine prayer, we stop performing, making excuses, or trying to prove something—to ourselves or to others—and we say what is really on our heart: our fears and hopes, our desires and sorrows, what hurts, and what we long for. It is from this kind of openness that the deepest inner changes begin.

Regular prayer does not change us overnight. The process unfolds gradually—often so quietly that we hardly notice it at first. Over time, a steady prayer practice reshapes our thoughts, feelings, reactions, and familiar patterns of behavior. Not in a single day, but step by step, it renews our inner world—making us more attentive to ourselves, more honest, and more deeply rooted.

Where Change Begins

Rarely does the need for change arise in a season of well-being: when everything feels fine, there is no reason to change. Almost always, the turning point comes through something difficult—illness, loss, confusion, loneliness. When external supports stop working, when familiar structures collapse, a person truly turns inward—and toward the Divine.

And prayer begins. Not because *"it's required,"* but because there is no other way.

From that moment, something new appears within—the humility without which spiritual growth is impossible. And real faith begins to awaken: the sense that life holds something greater than what can be seen or managed through control. This is not weakness, nor is it passive surrender. It is an honest admission:

"I don't know everything. I don't control everything. I am open. I am ready to change."

In that inner readiness, a possibility appears: movement, a way out of the impasse, a different life.

When you pray consciously, you begin to hear what you are actually saying—and to notice recurring themes. Which requests come back again and again? Which words do you speak automatically? What feelings are behind your prayer—fear, gratitude, shame, hope?

In moments like these, prayer becomes a mirror of the soul. It shows what you truly fear, what you are seeking, what you doubt, where you lose your footing. You learn to listen to yourself—and truly hear yourself—to understand what you really want. This kind of honesty can be unexpected and even painful, but it is exactly here that the first steps begin: toward inner maturity, greater awareness, and real change in your life.

How Prayer Shapes Character

The habit of regular prayer changes us not immediately, but steadily and inevitably. Just as water, drop by drop, wears away stone, prayer gradually opens a new space within the soul. Into that space comes quiet instead of irritation. Compassion instead of judgment. Trust instead of constant anxiety.

And one day, you notice that you respond to the same things differently. You rush less. You struggle less. You notice more—and observe more. Prayer teaches patience, humility, and honesty with yourself—not because you decided to "become a better person," but because you are drawing closer to the Divine Presence. And near the Source, the desire to be rude, petty, or greedy begins to fall away. There is less and less room inside for fear and inner restlessness.

True transformation is not a flash—it is a path: a simple, honest, daily practice. Prayer becomes a natural part of the day, like breathing: in the morning, to attune yourself; in the evening, to let go of what you've lived through; in difficult moments, so you don't break; in joyful ones, to give thanks.

This kind of prayer forms an inner center—calm, steady, alive. Even if something collapses in the outer world, you return to this space again and again. It already belongs to you —not as an idea, but as a lived experience.

This is spiritual discipline: not abandoning prayer even when it seems like it *"isn't working"*—because it is precisely in those seasons that it often works most deeply within you.

Prayer changes us not only through *"the right words,"* but also because, in those moments, we live from the heart. We touch what is real—warm and alive. We remember who we truly are. This contact—with the Source, with Silence, with Love—gradually changes everything.

You become different. You become yourself.

10

PRAYER AND INNER DIALOGUE

Each of us has an inner voice. Sometimes it sounds clear—almost like a narrator commenting on everything that happens to us. Sometimes it is barely noticeable, like a background hum we are hardly aware of. But it is always there.

We experience it as a stream of thoughts, but these are not just random phrases. This voice reflects our deepest beliefs: what we believe, what we consider right or wrong, and what we consider possible or impossible. In many ways, it shapes how we see ourselves, other people, God, and life itself.

The Nature of the Inner Voice

This voice forms very early. In childhood, we absorb the words of parents, teachers, and loved ones, and they take root within us, shaping our self-image and our view of the world. As we grow up, we continue to lean on our accumulated experience: what we once heard, felt, and lived through.

Sometimes our inner voice supports us and gives us the strength to move forward. But often it does the opposite: it stops us, judges us, and makes us anxious. The same phrases and inner scenarios repeat day after day—almost automatically, out of habit.

We get used to this continuous flow. It becomes part of us—so much so that we stop noticing it. But does it reflect who we really are? Most often, no. These are beliefs, fears, and other people's judgments that we have accumulated over time. They are not always fair, and sometimes they are not ours at all. And yet we allow them to play again and again. The more often inner criticism repeats, the deeper it takes root: we stop merely hearing it—we start believing it.

Sometimes this inner monologue sounds almost like a prayer—only a destructive one. Short phrases repeated day after day: *"Nothing will work out for me," "I'm unworthy," "Nobody loves me."* They become invisible affirmations. And if you repeat them—consciously or not—and believe them, they turn into a stable inner pattern that shapes your perception, your choices, your behavior, and ultimately your life.

But we have something that can change everything: the ability to notice our thoughts and choose our response. This is awareness. It allows us to pause, listen, and decide whether to keep living on autopilot—or to begin changing direction.

Once you recognize that much of life is shaped from within, the possibility of change appears. Because you can begin speaking to yourself differently. And one of the gentlest, most profound, and most effective ways to change the inner voice is through prayer.

How Prayer Changes Our Inner Dialogue

When prayer enters our lives, and we turn to it regularly, not only does what happens outside change, but also what sounds inside. The inner voice is transformed, the flow of thought shifts, the world begins to look different—and so do you within it.

Because prayer is not only a conversation with God. It is also a new way of speaking to yourself—in a different tone, with a different quality.

At first, the phrases of prayer can feel external, separate from your usual inner monologue. But if you pray sincerely and regularly, the words begin to sink in more deeply. They stop being memorized lines and become a living, breathing thing. They weave into the flow of thought and gradually change its rhythm, direction, and inner atmosphere.

What used to sound like, *"I've ruined everything again,"* is gradually replaced by, *"I'm learning. I'm trying. I'm walking my path."*

Instead of *"Nobody needs me,"* something new appears: *"I am not alone. I am heard. I matter."*

Instead of *"I am unworthy,"* comes: *"I am loved. I accept myself as I am."*

True prayer is a voice without judgment. It fosters trust, patience, kindness, and gratitude. First, you speak this way with the Divine—and then you begin to speak this way to yourself, because you and the Divine are inseparably connected.

Prayer does not silence inner criticism by force. It offers another possibility: another tone, another way of seeing yourself. It invites you to hear a different voice—a gentle, accepting voice that is not quick to condemn. And one day you may feel that this voice has become your own.

A Moment of Honesty: What Are You Saying When You Pray?

Sometimes it's essential to pause for a moment and ask yourself a simple but profound question: What am I saying right now—

and why am I praying? Yes, we turn to God. But what lies behind our words? What, exactly, are we trying to express through this form?

One of the foundations of effective prayer is our emotional state. What is in your heart right now—peace or fear, gratitude or pain, resentment or anxiety? Do you pray with confidence—or do you issue an ultimatum: *"Do this, or I won't be able to cope"*?

Sometimes we think we are speaking to the Divine, but in reality, it's a *"parental"* voice within us—childhood resentment, or the shadow of guilt—that is speaking. We say a prayer, but inside, the old pain, old patterns, and old scenarios go on.

In that moment, it's important to stop and listen: *"What do I truly want to say? What is behind my words?"*

This is the point of honesty. It is not a place for correction or self-criticism, but a space for sincere recognition: *"Where am I speaking from right now? Why do I feel these emotions? What drives them—habit, fear, the need to control everything?"*

True prayer begins here. Not with the *"right"* words, but with the moment you stop hiding, look inward, and ask yourself uncomfortable but important questions.

You stop playing the role of a *"good person"* or trying to earn blessings. You become yourself—exactly as you are right now. And you begin to see: where you are, who you are, what you truly feel.

In this honesty, a sense of Presence can suddenly appear—alive, warm, real. "*Yes, this is who I am. I accept myself as I am—right now."*

Because change is impossible until it becomes clear what, exactly, needs to be changed.

And then prayer stops being an empty formality. It becomes an encounter with God, with yourself, with truth.

Practicing a New Inner Voice

Changing your inner dialogue is not a quick process. Old words, familiar judgments, and automatic reactions have been echoing inside us for years. That is why it's important to consciously offer an alternative: new wording, a different tone, a different perspective.

This is not about ignoring pain or pretending that *"everything is fine."* It is about consciously noticing what you say to yourself and what you believe. And it is about regularly asking yourself: *"Is what I just thought true?" "Why do I keep finding myself around these kinds of people?" "Why do the same situations keep repeating in my life?"*

Notice the words you hear inside yourself, and try to replace them with others—gentle, supportive, simple ones. Let them first be spoken in prayer, and then let them begin to take root in everyday life.

It is like moving into a new home: quiet and warm, with windows facing the light. A home where you are heard, where it is safe to be yourself and to change without fear. But moving takes effort: letting go of what no longer serves you, and developing new supportive habits. One of them is regular, living prayer.

Practice words that continue to resonate inside you even after you have spoken them, like a warm echo. They can be simple phrases you return to again and again. Repeat them as a short affirming prayer or as a form of new inner dialogue—not *"because you have to,"* but because they bring peace to your soul. It is precisely these words that change your perception—your perception of yourself and the world around you:

I am surrounded by love. I feel supported and cared for. I am walking my path. I am unique—and that is my beauty. I am part of a greater plan.

Such phrases are like drops of light. If you allow them to

sound again and again, they gradually become part of your inner space—the very place where a new life begins.

Let your prayer be alive: not a ritual, but a conversation; not only a request, but a presence; not an escape from yourself, but a return to yourself.

11

PRAYER AND THE BODY

The soul needs the body to live in this world. Even when we pray, we are in the body, too. Although prayer may seem "non-physical," everything that happens within us is reflected in the body in one way or another: in our breathing, posture, facial expression, sensations, and sometimes even in our health.

The body is not just a physical shell. It is a living boundary between our inner self and external reality. It is the instrument through which, on the one hand, we come to know our soul, and on the other, we come into contact with life and the world around us. And when we pray, the body is always involved—even if we don't notice it.

The Body as a Vessel for the Soul

Sometimes we get too caught up in the mind, trying to *"pray correctly."* But deep prayer is born not only in thoughts and words, but also in how we breathe, how we sit, how we feel in the moment. A restless mind scatters attention. Tense muscles keep the heart from opening. And conversely, a soft, relaxed body helps prayer come alive.

To understand that the body participates in prayer is to begin paying attention to physical sensations—to stop ignoring them or pushing them away. It is to learn to listen to the body as an important source of inner connection: the connection between the soul and the Divine Presence.

Because what we call God touches us not only on a spiritual level, but also on a physical one: through trembling, warmth, lightness, tears, and peace. And if we learn to observe the body and consciously feel it, we can experience prayer not only with the mind and heart, but with the whole body as well.

Physical States and the Quality of Prayer

We often underestimate how much our physical condition affects the depth of prayer. Fatigue, tension, hurry, and physical pain reduce emotional sensitivity, distract attention, and get in the way of inner concentration. Conversely, calm breathing, relaxed shoulders, and a straight but gentle posture create a sense of inner space in which prayer can go deeper.

Your physical state is the background against which your inner music plays. And if that background is filled with anxiety, tension, or physical discomfort, the music will be disjointed and weak. But if the body is calm, breathing freely, and feeling safe, prayer becomes filled with softness, warmth, and presence.

You can feel this right now. Sit comfortably. Release tension in your neck, shoulders, and abdomen. Close your eyes. Take a few slow breaths in and out. Feel your breath. Notice how, with each exhale, a little more stillness settles within you. And then begin to pray—as you know how. Notice how different it feels, and how much clearer your turning to the Divine becomes.

This is the meaning of physical preparation: not mechanical discipline, but conscious care. You tune the instrument through which your soul speaks. You create an inner atmosphere in which prayer becomes alive, sincere, and deep. Sometimes, a few minutes of attention to the body before prayer can truly change everything.

Physical Practices as Preparation for Prayer

We can't always enter prayer with ease. Sometimes the mind is restless, the body is tense, and attention is scattered. In those moments, we need simple ways to return to ourselves—and physical practices can become a bridge between everyday life and a state of prayer.

It doesn't have to be anything complicated. Sometimes it is enough to stand up, do a few gentle bends, stretch, and roll your shoulders. These movements help release tension, bring you back into your body, and *"ground"* you. You can stand barefoot on the floor, feel the support beneath your feet, and take a deep breath. These simple actions draw you back to the here and now and tune you toward inner silence.

Breathing is one of the most accessible and powerful tools. A few minutes of slow, conscious breathing helps the mind calm down, the body relax, and the heart open. This is already the beginning of prayer—only without words.

Some people find mindful movement helpful: slow walking, gentle gestures, attention to each step. Others find light stretching, or even dancing, works for them. The key is not the form, but presence. In these moments, you are not *"working on your body"*—you are returning to yourself, to your center.

Such practices don't replace prayer; they prepare the ground. They are like opening a door—and behind it you are already waiting: yourself, your body, your heart, and the One to whom you turn. This is a way to involve your whole being in prayer: not only your mind and voice, but also your body—as a living participant in the encounter.

Simple Physical Rituals That Help You Enter Prayer

Over time, each person develops their own approach to prayer. But there are simple physical actions that can serve as *"gateways"* to a prayerful state. These are not necessarily rituals in the religious sense—they are habits that help you move from the outer world into yourself.

Washing your face or gently touching it. Water cleanses not only the body, but also the inner state. Simple washing can become a symbolic gesture: *"I leave the hustle and bustle of the day behind and enter a space of silence."* Even simply running your hands over your face and neck signals to the body that something different is about to begin.

An upright posture. Straightening your back, relaxing your shoulders, feeling your neck lengthen, and your chest gently open—this is not just a physical adjustment. It is a sign of openness—a gesture the body remembers: *"I am now connected to something greater."*

Feeling supported. Feel your feet on the floor. Feel how you are sitting or standing. Place your palm on your heart or stomach to restore a sense of presence: *"I am here."* In that moment, prayer is already beginning—even if you haven't yet spoken a word.

Gentle movement. Sometimes, to enter a prayerful state, it helps to make a few slow hand movements—as if opening yourself. These can be gestures of gratitude, acceptance, or silence. Anything that helps the body become part of the prayer.

A lit candle or a gentle scent. The flame of a candle or a gentle scent (incense or essential oil) engages the other senses. These things are not *"magical,"* but they create an atmosphere—and that atmosphere helps the soul relax, tune in, and open.

What matters is not what you do, but how you do it: with attention, respect, and presence. Keep your ritual genuine but straightforward. After all, the essence is not in the form, but in connection with yourself, with God, with the moment.

Prayer Within the Body: How It Feels

When we begin to pay more attention to the body during prayer, a wonderful experience gradually unfolds: prayer stops being only words—it becomes sensation. It can live within the body as clearly as breathing or the beating of the heart.

Some people feel prayer in the chest—as warmth, expansion, a subtle tingling. Some feel it in the belly—as a gentle heaviness, or, conversely, as a pleasant spaciousness. Sometimes prayer is felt in the palms—through a tremor, or through the impulse to open the hands. Some experience a quiet wave of calm, as if something is flowing out from within.

There is no *"correct"* form for these sensations. They don't always come immediately, and there is no need to invent them. What matters is not forcing anything, but noticing what the body is saying in its quiet language: *"I hear you. I am here. I am praying too."*

If, during prayer, you experience even a brief feeling of warmth or inner expansion, stay with it a little longer. Don't rush back into your head—to words and control. Breathe with the feeling. This is inner attunement: when prayer sounds not only in your thoughts, but also in your body. Then your whole being becomes part of the encounter—and you feel more whole.

A Unified Whole: Body, Mind, and Heart

Sometimes it can seem that the body is merely a tool that must be *"turned off"* to pray more deeply. But true prayer, on the contrary, gathers everything—mind, heart, and body—into a single whole.

Thoughts help us find words. The heart fills those words with meaning, love, and trust. And the body gives them the power of presence—through breath, warmth, and peace. If one of these elements is missing, prayer can become dry or mechanical. But when everything sounds together, it is alive.

Prayer is not only words addressed to the Divine. It is also your shoulders—lowered and relaxed. It is your breath—steady and gentle. It is your heart, which hears, feels, and responds. It is your body—one that does not hinder but helps.

Because in that moment, you are whole, alive, and fully present. Let your body be an ally, not an obstacle. Let your mind not wander; let it guide you deeper. Let your heart respond. And let every breath you take be a prayer.

12

FORMAL PRAYER

Formal prayer is when there are words, but no life in them—when a person repeats familiar phrases, follows an outer ritual, but inside there is emptiness or indifference.

It is important to note right away: this is not because a person is *"bad," "unbelieving,"* or *"lazy."* Most often, formal prayer is a form of self-protection. Sometimes it is simply easier to pray *"out of habit,"* just so as not to look deeper within, not to acknowledge what you truly feel, not to touch what hurts.

Formal prayer is like a beautiful wrapper with nothing inside. The words may be correct, even sublime, but if there is no genuine inner experience behind them—if the heart is silent—it remains only a form.

A person can check the box: *"I prayed, so everything is fine."* But inside, there is no real contact—neither with oneself nor with God.

It is like a mechanical *"I love you,"* said automatically, without any inner response. The phrase was spoken, but no one truly felt anything: neither the one who said it, nor the one it was said to.

Formal prayer is not frightening or *"sinful."* It is simply a signal: somewhere you have closed yourself off, gone into your head, and forgotten why you are doing this. If you have noticed it, that is already good. It means there is an opportunity to return to the living breath of prayer.

Why We Slip into Formality

Formal prayer rarely appears by accident. There are almost always reasons behind it.

First, **habit.**

If you recite the same texts for many years, attend church on a schedule, and repeat familiar formulas, the mind becomes accustomed to it. The words are learned and begin to come out on their own, without the involvement of the heart. This is a natural process: whatever is repeated often enough will sooner or later become automatic.

Second, **protection from pain.**

Living prayer always requires honesty. And honesty can be painful: to admit that I am afraid, envious, offended, disappointed; to admit that I don't understand God, that I am angry with Him, that I feel abandoned. It is much easier to recite a familiar text than to face what is true in me—before myself and before the Divine Presence.

Third, **the fear of "doing something wrong."**

Many people grew up in traditions where the main thing is not sincerity, but following the form: *"that's how it should be," "that's how it needs to be," "that's how it's always been done."* In such a system, it is easier to follow a ready-made template than to search for a living, personal language for addressing God.

And finally, **fatigue and inner burnout.**

Sometimes there is almost no strength left. Emotions are dulled. Inside, there is only a weary *"it is what it is."* In such periods, a person continues to pray out of inertia: because *"it is necessary,"* because it once helped, because it is frightening to admit, *"I don't feel anything right now."*

In all these cases, formal prayer is not a verdict, but a symptom. It says: *"I am tired. I am afraid. I am hiding."* This admission alone is already a step toward honesty.

Signs of Formal Prayer

How can you tell when prayer has become formal—*"dry"*?

- You are in a hurry. You want to skim the text, fulfill the *"norm,"* and move on with your life.
- The words leave no trace. You pray, and a minute later, you don't even remember what you said. Your soul doesn't feel lighter, clearer, or deeper.
- You *"report to God."* Inside, there is a sense of duty: *"I must pray, or else..."* But there is no sense of encounter, dialogue, or presence.
- You can't tolerate pauses. You want to *"finish"* as quickly as possible so as not to be alone with your own silence.
- You are afraid to go beyond the text. You don't allow yourself a single phrase of your own, a single word *"from yourself"*—only what is written in the prayer book.

If you recognize yourself in even a few of these, don't blame yourself. Say honestly: *"Yes, my prayer is more formal than alive right now."* And that is already the beginning of change.

The Danger of Remaining in Formal Prayer

Formal prayer can be a stage on the path, and that is okay. But if you remain in it for a long time, there are risks.

First, **disappointment.**

When a person prays *"correctly"* for years, but nothing changes inside, they may conclude, *"Prayer doesn't work. God doesn't hear me."* In reality, it is not prayer itself that fails—it is the form of prayer, detached from the heart.

Second, **spiritual pride.**

Sometimes outwardly pious but empty prayer creates an illusion: *"I'm doing everything right, so I'm a good believer."* Behind this may be an unwillingness to truly change—to face one's own fears and shadows.

Third, **alienation from yourself.**

If you often speak words that don't match your inner state, a split can form: one *"I"* is external and *"correct,"* while another is internal—alive, but hidden. Over time, it can become hard to know what you actually feel.

The main danger is not that God will be *"offended"* by formal prayer. The main danger is that we ourselves stop being alive in the process.

Formal Prayer as a Stage on the Path

And yet it is vital to understand that formal prayer is not always negative. Sometimes it is a necessary step.

Sometimes a person is going through a difficult time and feels emotionally drained. There is no inner strength, no honest words. Everything feels empty. In such a moment, they take a familiar text and read it out of habit. They feel hollow inside, but they still come. They still open the prayer book. They still say at least these words.

This is already a movement. This is already a memory of connection. Even if it is almost imperceptible right now, the very fact that a person does not abandon prayer matters.

The opposite can happen, too. At first, a person enters prayer through a formal ritual because it is the custom in their family or community. Over time, they begin to ask questions and search for their own language, their own way of addressing God. The formal form becomes a framework within which living content gradually emerges.

So the task is not to *"get rid of"* formal prayer, but not to stop there: to gradually bring the heart, attention, breath, and presence back into it.

The Transition from Formal Prayer to Living Prayer

How can we revitalize prayer that has become a formality?

- **Slow down.** Read the same words more slowly. Pause at least once and ask yourself: "*Do I really agree with what I am saying? How do I feel as I say this?*"
- **Add a word or two of your own.** You don't need to change the entire text immediately. But after the prayer, you can quietly add, *"Lord, right now I feel..."* and describe your current state.
- **Engage your body.** Take a deeper breath. Feel your chest. Notice your posture and your physical sensations. Sometimes it is enough to straighten your back and relax your shoulders—and the prayer already sounds different.
- **Allow yourself to be "imperfect" in prayer.** Don't strive to pray beautifully or *"properly."* Allow yourself to pray honestly: let your words reflect fatigue, irritation, even reluctance—but let them be true.

The transition from formal prayer to living prayer almost always begins with one step: honesty.

"I don't feel it.
I'm tired.
I pray out of habit.
But I want more.
I want to be alive in this again."

Don't Judge—Just Notice

The most important thing is not to turn this conversation about formal prayer into a new reason for self-condemnation. Formality is not a failure, but an invitation: to notice that somewhere you have lost touch with yourself—and to gently restore it.

If you notice that you are praying mechanically, you can say to God: *"I feel almost nothing right now. I'm saying these words out of habit. But somewhere deep down, I am still searching for You. Help me come alive inside."*

In that moment, formal prayer ceases to be formal. Because the essential thing returns: a living, honest soul that longs for encounter.

PART III

PRACTICE

13

FROM THEORY TO PRACTICE: PRAYER FORMS AND FINDING WHAT FITS

It is time to leave theoretical reflection behind and move into practice. If everything we have discussed so far remains only at the level of ideas, this book will not *have fulfilled* its purpose. Prayer is alive only when you practice it—when it becomes not just an abstract concept, but part of your day, your way of being, your path.

Every prayer is connected, in one way or another, to a spiritual tradition or religious system. I am familiar with many traditions; one of them is the Hawaiian tradition of Ho'oponopono. But in this part of the book, I will not offer a comparative review of religions and schools. What matters more to me is this: to help you find forms of prayer that will work in your life—with your experience, your character, your relationship to the Divine.

I want to clarify one point. Earlier, we spoke about three basic types of prayer (petitionary, thanksgiving, and affirming). Below, I will offer a more practical map: a set of prayer forms that show up in real life. They *don't* replace the basic types, but they help you see how prayer can sound in specific situations.

Different Forms of Prayer

From a theological perspective, there are many ways to classify prayer. Below, I offer a practical section to help you choose a form of prayer tailored to your life situation and experience.

A Prayer of Gratitude

This is a prayer in which you *don't* ask, complain, or bargain—you simply say, *"Thank you."*

In the endless flow of days, we often focus on problems and fail to notice what we can be grateful for. Here, it is important to be attentive and specific. *Don't* wait for something big. Every day, dozens of small things happen that we take for granted—and it is in these things that the quiet miracle of life often lives.

Every day there is an opportunity to give thanks: to yourself, your body, your loved ones, the people you encounter, and life itself. This kind of prayer clears the heart of chronic dissatisfaction, broadens perception, and reminds us that, no matter what, there is already light in your life.

A Prayer of Petition

This is the most familiar form of prayer for most people. We turn to the Divine when we are struggling or lacking something: health, strength, money, support, wisdom.

In a prayer of petition, what matters is not only what you say, but also the inner state from which you turn to God: from fear, or from trust? From the feeling *"I am owed,"* or from an inner openness: *"May what serves the highest good come."*

It is important to understand that there are no secrets between you and the Divine. God knows what you need even before you put it into words. A prayer of petition is not an attempt to *"persuade"* some capricious force to intervene in your life. It is a way to honestly see your needs, acknowledge your limitations, name what matters—and trust that there is Wisdom and Power greater than your personal self.

This prayer becomes especially profound when you ask not only for external things (*"give me...," "fix this..."*), but also for inner qualities: clarity, patience, courage, the ability to see the next step. Very often, we need not so much a ready-made solution as the ability to see what to do next.

A simple guideline is this: ask for what helps you and others live with more love, clarity, and inner freedom. And phrase your request so it sounds not like panic, but like trust:

"Calm my soul, grant me clarity, and show me my next step. I am open to your help and ready to take that step."

A Prayer of Repentance and Healing

This is a prayer we come to when we feel guilt, shame, pain, or resentment—toward ourselves, toward others, toward life, and sometimes even toward the Divine. It is not about self-humiliation or *"beating ourselves up"* for *our* mistakes. True repentance is inner honesty and a willingness to change.

At the heart of such a prayer is acknowledgment:

"Yes, I went wrong somewhere... and now I want to live differently."

Repentance is a turning point—a change of direction. You stop making excuses and begin to take responsibility for your thoughts, words, and actions.

A prayer of healing begins when you bring your pain into the light of God's presence. You *don't* hide it or pretend that *"everything is fine."* You name what hurts, what disturbs you, what wounds you carry inside.

It is important to ask not only for unpleasant feelings to go away, but also for inner reconciliation with yourself, for a softening of the heart, for the ability to forgive—yourself, others, and life. Simple words are often more powerful here than the *"right"* ones:

"I acknowledge what happened. I am sorry. Heal in me what led to this. Help me move forward with greater love and wisdom."

A classic example of this kind of prayer (if you are familiar with *it*) is Ho'oponopono. The phrases:

"I'm sorry. Please forgive me. Thank you. I love you."

are not a magic formula, but a way to take responsibility for your inner *state*, cleanse your inner space, and step out of the cycle of mutual grievances—real or imagined.

A Prayer of Intention (Creative, Affirmative)

This is a prayer in which you set the direction of your life: where you want to go, who you want to become, and what qualities you want to develop in yourself.

Here, it is essential to distinguish between desire and intention. A desire often sounds like, *"I want everything to go my way."* An intention is more like an inner decision to live in harmony with deeper values: love, wisdom, honesty, beauty.

In such a prayer, you not only ask, but also affirm:

"I choose... I open myself... I intend..."

You name not only an external result, but the inner state in which you want to live. For example:

"I intend to live with greater trust and less fear. I choose to see paths

and possibilities in my life. I open myself to letting love, wisdom, and kindness shine through me."

It is important that these words are alive. A short but honest phrase you can believe—even a little—is better than a long, beautiful text that *doesn't* resonate with you.

And one more thing: creative prayer leaves room for higher wisdom. You can clearly state your intention and then add inwardly:

"May this be fulfilled in the form that serves the highest good—for me and for others."

Then intention *doesn't* turn into control; it becomes cooperation with the Divine.

A Prayer of Presence (Quiet, Contemplative)

This is a prayer in which there are fewer words and deeper attention. Here, you formulate almost nothing. You simply remain in the presence of the Divine—as if sitting quietly beside Someone dear to you. You can begin with a short phrase to set the tone:

"I am here. You are here. I am in Your presence."

Then let go of words and remain with the feeling. If thoughts come, *don't* fight them—gently return your attention to your breath, to your heart, to the quiet sense of Presence.

Over time, this prayer becomes a *source of support*: you begin to return to it not only in silence, but in the middle of daily life.

A Prayer for Others (Intercessory)

This is a prayer in which you turn to God on behalf of your loved ones and those who are going through hardship.

It is important to understand that you are not *"breaking"* another person's freedom or trying to *"push through"* the result you want. You simply hold the person in light and trust, and you remember that Divine wisdom knows their path more deeply than you do.

A very simple form:

"I bring (name) to You. You know what they are going through right now. I ask for light, protection, and support for them. May what serves the highest good unfold—for them and for everyone around them."

And one more thing: when you pray for others, you *don't* take responsibility for the outcome. You open your heart, bring the person into your prayer—and then you let go.

A Prayer of Trust and Acceptance

This prayer arises where our strength and explanations end:

"Your will be done."
"I don't understand, but I trust."

It becomes especially important when the situation does not change despite requests and effort; when answers *don't* come, or come in a different form than you expected. This is a prayer of inner agreement:

"I remain with You, even if it is hard for me right now. Even if I do not understand."

It is important not to confuse this with passive *resignation*. It is not, *"Do whatever You want with me."* It is an honest admission:

"I have done everything I could at my level, and now I choose to trust the One who sees further and deeper."

You *don't* stop acting—you stop fighting reality from within. You can say directly:

"I'm scared. I'm hurting. I don't understand where this is leading. But I choose to stay with You. Help me go through this with as much love, wisdom, and honesty as I can muster."

These forms should not be taken as a rigid framework. In real life, one prayer can include gratitude and request, repentance and healing, trust and intention all at once. This *"map"* is simply a tool to help you understand what you are doing when you pray—and what is closest to you *right now*.

A Map of Prayer Modalities

Every prayer has not only a "*type*" (what it is about), but also a **modality**—an emotional tone and inner direction: how it sounds from within. Several basic modalities can be distinguished:

- **Praise:** admiration and recognition of the greatness of the Divine.
- **Request:** *"help," "protect," "give."*
- **Gratitude:** *"thank you"*—for support, lessons, and joys.
- **Repentance/confession:** honest admission and a willingness to live differently.

- **Blessing:** speaking good into life—your own or someone else's.
- **Trust and acceptance:** the shift from control to agreement.
- **Silent listening:** the willingness not to speak, but to hear.

The same type of prayer can be expressed through different modalities. For example, a request expressed in fear might sound like: "

Do something, or I won't be able to bear it."

A request expressed in trust might sound like:

"This is hard for me, but I am in Your hands. Show me how to go through this with wisdom."

Choosing a Prayer in Different Situations

Now, on to the most practical *part*. There is no single *"right"* prayer for all occasions. But there are a few guidelines that can help you *find your way*.

When you are afraid and anxious, prayers of trust and protection can be especially helpful:

"I am in Your hands. Help me feel supported. Give me clarity and show me the next step."

When you feel guilt, shame, or resentment, this is a space for repentance and healing. Ho'oponopono often works well here.

When you are confused and *don't* understand how to proceed, prayers of intention and clarity are appropriate:

"Show me the next step. Help me see the truth. Give me the wisdom to discern."

When you ask for external changes, *don't* let your request turn into an ultimatum. It is better to say:

"I really want this. If it serves the highest good, help it come to pass. If not, help me accept another path."

When everything is relatively calm, gratitude is especially important. It strengthens the connection and keeps the heart from *"falling asleep"* when there is no crisis.

When you feel joy and fulfillment, praise and thanksgiving come naturally:

"Thank You for life. Thank You for the opportunity to love and be loved."

Why Do You Need All This?

This part of the book is not about memorizing classifications and repeating them like a chart. It is about putting together your own personal set of prayers—one that is alive and useful in everyday life.

Next, in the "Practice" section, we will talk about:

- what morning and evening prayer might look like;
- how to pray in moments of fear, loss, and pain;
- how to use gratitude as daily support;
- how to practice prayers of forgiveness (including through Ho'oponopono);

- how to build your personal rhythm of prayer—day by day, week by week.

Theory matters: it gives us understanding, language, and structure. But practice is what makes prayer a real, effective tool in everyday life.

14

MORNING AND EVENING PRAYER: A PERSONAL PRAYER RHYTHM

Moving from theory to practice, it is important to understand one simple thing: prayer is not a one-time event, but a rhythm of life.

It is not necessary to pray for hours, go to a monastery, or radically change your lifestyle. What matters more is creating a few anchor points in your day—moments when you consciously turn your attention inward, notice your emotional state, and return to yourself and to the Divine Presence.

Most often, these points naturally fall in the morning and in the evening. Morning is like setting the tone before the day begins. Evening is like taking stock and consciously letting the day go.

This chapter is about how you can build your personal prayer rhythm without disrupting your life—gently weaving prayer into the life you already live.

Why Do We Need a Prayer Rhythm?

Our minds are designed to forget quickly. This is especially noticeable in our time, when events flash by like a kaleidoscope and news and problems pour in every day. Even the most profound insights and the most vivid experiences dissolve in the hustle and bustle of work, phone calls, tasks, and worries.

A rhythm of prayer is not necessary *"to please God"* or *"to earn blessings."* It is essential, first and foremost, for you—in order to:

- not lose your inner axis and peace amid the outer *noise*;
- remember more often that your life is not only about problems and responsibilities, but also about support, meaning, and Presence;
- gradually fill your days with a different quality of attention, different emotions, a different *way of seeing* what is happening.

As you slowly change yourself—your habits and your inner world—you gain the opportunity to live differently. A rhythm of prayer helps these changes become part of your everyday experience, rather than remaining only a beautiful idea.

Morning and evening prayers are like two shores of the same day. Your life flows between them. And how you begin and end your day largely determines how that day will feel.

Morning Prayer: How to Set Yourself Up for the Day

Mornings are often like a small storm: alarm clocks, rushing, children, traffic, news, and messages. It is very easy to dive headfirst into worries, plans, and control.

Morning prayer is a few minutes in which you first tune in to your inner state—and only then "turn on" the day. This can take very little time: three to five minutes of silence, a few simple words, one deep breath with a conscious *turning inward.*

What matters is not the *amount* of time, but the quality of presence.

Morning prayer can include three simple elements.

1. *Awareness of presence.* Pause for a moment and acknowledge: "I am not alone. I am not living this day in emptiness. The Divine Presence is already here, right beside me."
2. *Intention for the day.* Remember how you want to live this day inwardly—with what support and what attitude. Not "what I must accomplish," but "how I want to be in the situations that arise."
3. *Trust and a request for support.* Calmly acknowledge that you *don't* control everything, and ask for help where things feel difficult, unclear, or troubling.

This can be expressed in straightforward words. For example:

"Lord, I enter this day with You. I don't know everything, and I don't control everything, but I trust that You are guiding me. Help me today to see more clearly, to hear my heart, not to give in to fear and irritation, but to choose trust and gratitude. May everything that happens to me today serve the highest good—for me and for those I meet."

It is not necessary to repeat these exact words. What matters is that you recognize yourself in the prayer—that it contains your intention, your concerns, your hope.

Evening Prayer: Taking Stock and Letting Go

If morning prayer is about setting the tone, evening prayer is about speaking with God about what has already happened. In the evening, we often feel:

- fatigue;
- the feeling that *"I didn't get everything done again"*;
- regret about what was said—or left unsaid;
- anxiety about what tomorrow will bring.

Evening prayer helps us not carry all of this into sleep. It is meant to:

- *give thanks for the day that has passed;*
- *acknowledge your mistakes without beating yourself up;*
- *give to God what you can no longer change;*
- *ask for peace, restoration, and forgiveness.*

Evening prayer can also be divided into several steps.

Recall the day. Briefly review the main events in your mind: who you spoke with, what you did, and what you thought about.

Gratitude. Find at least two or three moments for which you can sincerely say "thank you": for a smile, for help, for a lesson, for something that worked out, or simply for making it through a difficult day.

Acknowledge difficulties and mistakes. Be honest:

"Here, I said too much. Here I shut down. Here I was afraid. Here I fell into an old habit again."

Not for self-condemnation, but for clarity.

Forgiveness and letting go. Ask forgiveness from God, from people (inwardly), from yourself. And consciously let the day go:

"I did everything I could. The rest is in Your hands."

A request for peace. Ask for inner rest and restoration—for the night to become a time of emotional healing and peace, not only physical sleep.

Example of an evening prayer:

"Lord, I thank You for this day. Thank You for everything good and kind in it today, and for the difficult moments—through them, I learn. I admit that I haven't always managed to remain calm, and that it hasn't always been easy to be patient and attentive. Forgive me where I have hurt others or myself— by word, by thought, or by inaction. I let go of what I can no longer change, and I entrust to You what still worries me. Fill my night with peace, my heart with silence and love, and my tomorrow with light and meaning. Let it be so. Amen."

You can change the words, change the meaning, and adapt it to yourself. What matters is that your emotional state is reflected in it—and gradually dissolves in it: gratitude for what was, forgiveness of yourself and those who hurt you, trust in the Divine Presence, and faith in tomorrow.

"I Don't Have Time" and Other Common Objections

Very often, a familiar thought pops up: *"That's all well and good, but I don't have time. In the morning, I'm in a rush, and in the evening, I'm tired."*

I understand this reaction. But it is important to notice one thing: it is not about duration, but about attention.

Morning prayer can take a minute—on the way to the shower, over a cup of tea, on the way to the car. Evening prayer can be said when you are already lying in bed and have turned off the light.

Even if, in the morning, you say, *"Lord, I enter this day with You,"* and, in the evening, *"Lord, I thank You for this day. Help me rest," that* is already a rhythm.

What matters most is consistency and regularity: consciously returning your attention to yourself, your body, your emotional state, and your connection with the Divine Presence.

Your prayer *doesn't* have to be long to be real. Sometimes the most profound thing is one honest sentence spoken from the heart, rather than ten pages read automatically.

How to Find Your Format

For some, morning prayer happens at the breakfast table in the quiet. For others, it happens behind the wheel on the way to work. For some, it is in the bathroom while the house is still asleep.

For some, evening prayer is a few words in a journal. For others, it is a quiet whisper before bed. For some, it is a walk outside after dark.

There are no *"right"* or *"wrong"* options here. There is only one question:

In what format is it easiest for me to be honest with myself and truly present?

You can ask yourself a few questions:

- When during the day is it easiest for me to *find* at least a couple of minutes of silence?

- How is it easiest for me to speak to God—out loud, in a whisper, inwardly, or by writing it down?
- Which words are closer to me—ready-made texts, or my own, even if they are *rough* and imperfect?

The answers to these questions will help you gradually shape your own personal morning and evening ritual.

A Little Agreement with Yourself

You can treat this as a small experiment. Not as a strict vow to *"pray every day from now on,"* but as an inner agreement: *"I will try, for at least a week or two, to begin and end each day with a short but sincere prayer. And I will see what changes."*

Most likely, outwardly, almost nothing will change at first. But inside, a new feeling will begin to emerge—as if your day is not only a set of tasks, but part of a larger journey.

And then morning and evening prayer will stop feeling like a *"spiritual obligation." They will* become your personal movement toward the Divine—toward the One who is always moving toward you.

In the following chapters, we will talk in more detail about how to pray in difficult moments, how to use prayers of gratitude and forgiveness, and how, based on all of this, you can create your own personal prayers—the ones your heart will want to return to.

15

PRAYER IN DIFFICULT MOMENTS: FEAR, PAIN, UNCERTAINTY

There are times when it feels easy to talk about prayer: a quiet evening, a cup of tea, a calm conversation, a simple sense of gratitude for the day that has passed.

And then there are other moments—when everything inside you tightens with fear; when a diagnosis arrives, betrayal strikes, or loss comes; when life changes beyond recognition in a matter of hours; when you look into the future and see only emptiness and fog, not a single clear step forward.

It's in moments like these that the question of prayer becomes especially urgent. How do you pray when you have no strength? When you're afraid? When everything inside you is screaming—or, on the contrary, goes numb?

This chapter is about prayer without *"getting it right."* Prayer at the edge of what we can bear—when words break, your voice trembles, and there are more questions than answers inside.

When the Soul Cannot Contain What Is Happening

In difficult moments, our psyche does what it knows how to do: it protects itself.

Some people go into denial: *"This can't be happening."* Some retreat into control: they begin frantically searching for solutions, options, schemes, and plans. Some freeze: they go numb inside, feeling neither pain nor tears. Some fall into despair and panic.

And then another layer can appear:

- *"I must pray correctly."*
- *"I have to hold on."*
- *"I must not complain."*
- *"I must believe."*
- *"I have to be strong."*

But in moments like these, the last thing we need is the *"right prayer."* We need a *living* prayer—one in which you can be exactly as you are right now: with fear, anger, confusion, and not knowing.

The Divine Presence does not need your reverence. It needs your truth.

Acknowledge Where You Are Before God

The most honest starting point in difficult moments can be very simple:

"Lord, I am afraid. I don't understand what's happening. I don't know what to do. But I still turn to You."

This is already a prayer—even if it contains not a single *"correct"* formula. In these words, you acknowledge:

- I can't handle this by myself;
- I don't control everything;
- I need *support* greater than myself.

Sometimes that's all you have the strength to do: to sit or lie there and whisper:

"I'm scared... stay with me."
"I'm in pain... don't leave me."
"I don't know how to go on...
but I'm still talking to You."

This is not a weakness. This is the inner turning we talked about in the chapter on transformation: from *"I have to do everything myself"* to *"I am not alone."*

Prayer in the Face of Fear

Fear is one of the most powerful emotions. It narrows perception, cuts off access to clear thinking, and forces us to see only the worst-case scenarios.

The first task of prayer in the face of intense fear is not to solve everything, but to widen your inner space just enough so you can breathe and think again. In that moment, it helps to:

- slow your breathing;
- feel your body (your feet, your hands, your breath);
- say a few very simple phrases.

For example:

"Lord, I feel intense fear. You know what I'm going through right now. Help me with this fear. Calm my soul. Show me my next step. Light my path. I'm not asking for a miracle right now— I'm asking for support here and now."

It can be even simpler:

"Lord, be with me in my fear. I am in Your hands, even if I cannot feel them right now."

Often, in moments of fear, we don't have the strength for long prayers. You can choose one or two phrases and repeat them like breathing:

"You are with me."
"I am in Your hands."
"Help me endure."

This is not a magic formula. It is a way to stay connected until the fear loosens its grip and makes room for the next step.

Prayer in Pain and Loss

There are moments when fear is joined by pain—or even replaced by it: loss, illness, betrayal, the collapse of hopes and expectations.

At times like these, honesty matters most. God does not need your forced smile or borrowed optimism. With Him, you can be completely real. He can hold your tears, your anger, even your accusation: *"Where were You when this happened?"*

Prayer in pain can begin as protest—what many traditions call a lament:

"Lord, this hurts so much. I don't understand why this is happening.

Part of me wants to scream and reject everything. I don't feel You. But I'm still speaking to You. Just help me get through this day. Help me breathe when it feels like I can't."

Sometimes your prayer is only a few words:

"I feel hurt."
"I'm scared for someone I love."
"It hurts to see this."

That doesn't ruin prayer. If anything, it makes it real.

And then, when the pain softens even a little, there may be room for words like these:

"If possible, ease the suffering. If this cannot be changed, help me go through it without losing myself— and without losing my love."

Remember: prayer in deep pain does not have to be wise or polished. It can be angry, messy, even contradictory. The important thing is to stay connected to the Divine Presence rather than shutting down into silence and isolation.

Prayer in Uncertainty

Uncertainty is its own kind of exhaustion. Nothing terrible has happened yet—but waiting for what might happen can drain you.

You're waiting for test results. A court decision. A response at work. The outcome of a difficult conversation.

In seasons like this, prayer can turn into bargaining:

"Make everything turn out okay. Only this way. Only according to my plan."

That's human. But if you *stay* stuck there, the inner tension usually only grows. Here it helps to gently shift your prayer from ultimatum to trust:

"Lord, You know how much I want this to go a certain way..." (and here you can honestly name what you want.) "I'm not letting go of this desire. But I admit I don't see the whole picture. If what I want truly serves my highest good, let it come to pass. If not, help me accept a different outcome without hardening my heart. Give me peace while I wait— and the strength to receive whatever comes."

This kind of prayer doesn't cancel your human desires. It simply creates space around them—a space for trust. You remember that not everything depends on you, and you choose to stay connected to the Divine Presence.

When You Can't Pray at All

Sometimes, in difficult moments, prayer feels impossible. The words won't come. Your heart feels like stone. Your mind shuts down—or becomes so loud you can't hold on to a single thought.

In times like this, you can do something very simple:

- Sit or lie down in a comfortable position.
- Place your hand on your chest or your stomach.
- Breathe for a few minutes, gently following each inhale and exhale.

And quietly say:

"I know You are near.
Calm my soul.
Surround me with Your love."

Or even:

"Lord, save me and keep me..."

Sometimes that is the only form of prayer available. And it is enough.

Remember: prayer is not only words. It is the intention to remain connected to the Divine Presence, even when you feel nothing at all.

Prayer as "First Aid"

You can think of prayer in difficult moments as spiritual first aid.

First aid doesn't heal everything at once. It doesn't replace doctors, treatment, or decisions. But it helps you take the next step.

In the same way, prayer doesn't always remove the problem. But it can give you strength to endure, calm your breathing, restore the sense that *"I'm not alone,"* and keep you from tearing yourself apart with panic, hatred, or despair.

Sometimes the core of a *"first-aid prayer"* sounds like this:

"Lord, don't let me grow bitter.
Help me stay alive inside,
even if everything around me is falling apart."

When There's No Answer in Sight

In hard seasons, silence can feel especially painful. You pray, you ask, you cry—and nothing changes on the outside.

As we said earlier, the answer to prayer doesn't always come in the form of a *"miracle on demand."* Sometimes it shows up in quieter ways:

You don't snap where you would have snapped before. Someone unexpectedly shows up for you. You feel a little calmer than yesterday. The situation doesn't get worse, even though it could have.

Try not to rush to the conclusion, *"God doesn't hear me."* Sometimes the very ability to stay steadier, not to lash out at the people you love, to keep your clarity and faith—that is prayer at work within you.

And you can say honestly:

"I don't see an answer. But I choose to keep speaking with You— even in this silence, even in this not-knowing."

In that moment, your prayer becomes not only a request, but *an act of* faithfulness: you stay in the dialogue, even when the easiest thing would be to quit.

Instead of a Conclusion

Prayer in difficult moments isn't about beautiful form. It isn't about *"being spiritual enough"* or looking strong.

It's about choosing not to break the living connection between you and the Divine Presence. About refusing to seal yourself off completely inside your pain. About not letting fear, grief, or uncertainty steal your sense of Presence.

Sometimes the best prayer sounds like this:

"I don't know how to go on.
But I don't want to go through this alone.
So I'm still speaking to You, Lord.
Hold me as You can.
And I will try not to let go of Your hand.
Calm my soul, show me the way,
support me in my grief."

If, in the hardest moments, you can hold on to even that thin thread, the rest will slowly begin to change shape.

Not always the way you expected. Not always the way you wanted.

But when you settle even a little and begin to watch more closely—what is changing within you, and around you—you may begin to see, or at least to feel, an answer.

In the next chapters, we will talk about how prayers of gratitude can support you even in adverse circumstances, and how prayers of forgiveness can free the heart from long-held burdens—so there is room for light again.

16

PRAYER OF GRATITUDE AND ABUNDANCE: A DAILY PRACTICE

After talking about prayer in fear and pain, it's important to name something that can support you not only in crisis, but every day: gratitude.

When we hear the word prayer, we usually think of asking:

"Lord, help me... give me... protect me..."

—or of repentance:

"Forgive me, Lord..."

But there is another kind of prayer that often stays in the background, even though it can radically change our inner state: **the prayer of gratitude.**

Why Gratitude Is Also a Prayer

Gratitude is not just a polite *"thank you."* It is a state in which you consciously notice that there is already light, support, resources, and love in your life—and you respond from the heart, even when it isn't easy.

A prayer of gratitude is a conversation with the Divine Presence that sounds like this:

"I see the good that is already here.
I acknowledge it.
I value it.
I give thanks for it."

Gratitude is the moment when your attention shifts from what is missing to what is already present. And as your attention shifts, the tone of your prayer changes. We stop being only petitioners and become participants in a living exchange: we receive—notice—give thanks—and begin to see more deeply.

Abundance Is More Than Money

When we hear the word abundance, the mind often jumps straight to material images: money, possessions, pleasure, comfort. There's nothing wrong with that—the material side of life matters.

But abundance is much broader than that. Abundance is when your life includes:

- people who bring you warmth and peace;
- time for small and big joys;
- health, strength, and opportunity;
- ideas, interest, and inspiration;
- an inner sense of meaning that keeps you from sinking into emptiness and despair.

A prayer of gratitude helps you recognize this fullness of life—even when some areas are still painful or unresolved. Not to deny reality, but to stop living with a constant sense of *lack*: *"This is missing. That is lacking..."*

Where there is gratitude, abundance often shows itself more naturally—not because we *"attracted"* something through a magic technique, but because we are consciously changing the way we relate to life.

Gratitude and Request: The Two Wings of Prayer

One important point: a prayer of gratitude does not cancel a prayer of request. It balances it. A request without gratitude can slowly turn into spiritual bargaining:

"Do what I want—or I'll be disappointed."

And gratitude without an honest request can become an escape from reality: *"Everything is fine,"* even when there is pain inside and a real need for change.

Real prayer stands on two *legs*:

- gratitude for what already exists;
- a sincere request for what has not yet come.

And gratitude makes the request gentler. Instead of:

"Do it already—how long do I have to wait?"

a different kind of prayer appears:

"Lord, thank You for everything I already have in my life. And along with that, I truly ask... If this will serve the highest good, please help it come to pass. And if not, show me another way."

A Daily Practice: Morning Gratitude Prayer

Morning is a wonderful time to begin the day with gratitude—not by checking the news, not by stepping straight into anxiety, but with one simple, conscious thought: *"I see and acknowledge how much I already have."*

In the morning, you can say a short prayer, for example:

"Lord, thank You for this new day. For the gift of being alive—for being able to breathe, see, and feel. Thank You for the people in my life, for my home, for food, for the chance to live, to learn, and to receive both small joys and great ones. I don't understand everything, but I know what my heart is reaching for. And I receive what I already have with gratitude. Thank You for this."

This prayer may take only one or two minutes. But if you practice it regularly, your emotional and mental baseline will begin to shift. The day will start not with a sense of lack, but with an awareness of the good that is already present—and gratitude for it.

Evening Gratitude: Gathering the Light of the Day

In the evening, it's much easier to remember what didn't work out: where you fell short, where you ran out of time, where everything went *"wrong"* again. By the end of the day, we're tired, and many things start to look darker than they really are.

An evening prayer of gratitude is a way to gather the light of the day, even if the day was hard. It helps you return your attention to what went well, and to what was still good, after all.

You can do this very simply. Recall two or three moments you can genuinely say *"thank You"* for:

- someone supported you;
- you handled a small task;
- you had a few minutes of peace;
- you did something that used to feel harder.

Then say it out loud—or quietly in your heart:

"Lord, thank You for the good that was in today. Thank You for... (name specific things). Thank You for the lessons of this day, even when they were not easy. I place in Your hands everything that didn't work out, and I thank You for helping me get through it."

The more specific you are, the deeper your gratitude becomes. Not only *"thank You for everything,"* but:

"Thank You for that conversation.
For that smile.
For that unexpected opportunity.
For the pause that kept me
from saying something foolish."

When It's Hard to Be Thankful

Honestly, there are days when gratitude feels almost impossible—when everything inside *you* protests: *"What is there to be thankful for? Everything is bad. Everything is falling apart. I'm scared, and I'm hurting."*

In moments like these, don't force yourself into fake thank-yous. True prayer always begins with truth. You can say:

"Lord, it is very hard for me to find words of gratitude right now. I see more pain than joy, more loss than gifts. It's hard for me to say 'thank You' sincerely. But I ask You: help me, in time, to see meaning in what

is happening— and to notice at least small glimmers of good, even in this season of my life."

And if you can find even one small thing to be grateful for, that is already enough. Sometimes it's something very simple: a cup of warm tea, a ray of sunlight, someone's gentle look—or even the fact that you can still turn toward God.

Gratitude "in Advance"

There is another important *form* of gratitude: you can be grateful not only for what has already happened—for the past—but also for what is still on the way, for what has not yet shown up in your life.

This isn't about *"forcing"* God to do what you want. It's about trusting the process—trusting that the Divine Presence is caring for you even when you cannot yet see how.

This kind of gratitude doesn't cancel action or replace real steps. It changes the inner ground from which you take those steps. Sometimes we lack clarity, but we can still choose trust and faith. A prayer like this might sound:

"Lord, thank You for the good that is already moving toward me, even if I cannot see it yet. Thank You for the opportunities that have not yet opened, for the meetings that have not yet happened, for the answers still ahead. I welcome all of this with trust and gratitude."

The key here is not to push reality, but to open yourself to the future—knowing that this path can also carry meaning and good, even if it doesn't look that way right now.

Gratitude and the Theme of Abundance

When gratitude becomes a regular practice, your relationship with abundance begins to change. You start to:

- compare yourself less with others;
- live less from the feeling of *"I never have enough"*;
- notice more often that you already have more than you thought.

And the paradox is this: from that state, it becomes easier to move forward—to look for new opportunities, to grow, to earn, to create. Not from panic and scarcity, but from steadier ground: the good that is already present in your life.

A prayer for material abundance can sound very different when it includes gratitude:

"Lord, thank You for what I already have: for a roof over my head, for food, for the people around me, for everything that sustains me today. You know my material needs, my fears about the future, and my desires. I ask for provision—for financial freedom, for new opportunities. If it serves the highest good, help me find the paths and the people through whom this can come. And at the same time, help me not to lose gratitude for what I already have right now."

Here the desire for well-being is not denied. But at the center is no longer greed or panic—it is a life lived in dialogue with the Divine Presence.

A Small Daily Step

To make gratitude prayer part of your life, begin with something simple. Choose a form that fits you:

- In the morning: name three things you're grateful for out loud.
- In the evening: write down three to five things in a notebook and end the day with a short prayer.
- During the day: pause at least once and say: *"Thank You for this moment. I see it, and I'm grateful for it."*

What matters most is regularity, not scale. Let it be a small practice—but a daily one. Over time, you'll notice that the habit of giving thanks changes not only your prayer but also the way you see life.

And this may be one of the most accessible paths to real abundance: when there is more light than darkness within you, more trust than complaint, more *"thank You"* than *"why is everything so bad?"*

In the next chapters, we will talk about prayers of forgiveness and healing—how prayer can free the heart from heavy feelings, and why, without this inner work, there often simply isn't room for gratitude and abundance.

17

PRAYER FOR FORGIVENESS AND HEALING: HO'OPONOPONO

Forgiveness is one of the most complex themes in spiritual practice. People talk about it a lot. It's often preached. But in real life, this is precisely where the most pain, resistance, and confusion tend to live.

On the one hand, we sense it: without forgiveness, the soul grows heavy and closed. Resentment accumulates. Anger builds. A lingering sense of injustice settles in.

On the other hand, you can't forgive *"on command."* Sometimes it can feel as if forgiving means agreeing with what happened—telling yourself, *"So it's okay to treat me this way. Everything is fine. Nothing terrible happened."* And something inside you refuses.

This chapter is about prayers that can help you change your relationship with the past—release situations whose memories weigh on your soul—and gradually loosen the burden you carry: resentment, guilt, shame, unfinished stories.

It's also about how the Hawaiian spiritual practice of Ho'oponopono can support this kind of healing.

Why Resentment Interferes with Prayer

Imagine your heart as a vessel through which love, gratitude, and trust can flow—the very energy from which prayer is born. When the heart is filled with old grievances, unspoken tears, and long-held bitterness, that vessel slowly clogs.

The words of prayer may still be spoken, but inside, there is no space for them to breathe. Everything feels tight—because there are too many hardened *"knots"* of pain we keep holding onto.

Resentment is stuck *energy*: something in the past that was never fully lived through, acknowledged, or released. We return to it again and again in our thoughts: *"How could he...?" "Why did they do that to me...?" "If only back then..."*

A prayer of forgiveness is not about saying, *"Everything was right,"* or *"I wasn't hurt."* It's about something else:

"Yes, it hurt. Yes, it was unfair. But I don't want to live inside that scene every day anymore. I want to step out of this cycle."

As long as we cling to resentment, a significant part of our life energy isn't available for the present, much less for the future. It stays stuck in the past. Forgiveness is one way we reclaim that energy.

Forgiveness Is Not Justification

It's crucial to separate two very different things: forgiving and justifying (or agreeing).To forgive does not mean saying, *"You did everything right. That's how it should have been."*

To forgive means saying:

"What happened was painful. It was wrong. It was unfair. But I no

longer want to carry this inside me. I choose to release you—or this situation—from my inner world. I am reclaiming my peace, my confidence, and my joy. I am healing myself."

Forgiving does not mean forgetting. Forgiveness does not erase boundaries, and it does not require you to restore trust. Forgiveness is, first and foremost, an act of care for yourself—for your heart, your soul, and your future.

Ho'oponopono: A Prayer of Cleansing and Responsibility

One practice that has remained alive and deeply meaningful for me over many years is the Hawaiian spiritual tradition of Ho'oponopono. In its simplest form, it is expressed in four phrases:

" I'm sorry.
Please forgive me.
Thank you.
I love you. "

At first glance, a natural question arises: *"What does this have to do with me? I was the one who was hurt. Why should I say 'forgive me'?"*

The meaning of Ho'oponopono is not to take someone else's guilt upon yourself. It's something different: *" I acknowledge my responsibility for what is happening inside me—for my reactions, my patterns, my unhealed wounds. "*

When I repeat these phrases, it is as if I am speaking to myself, to the Divine Presence, and sometimes to the person or situation through which my pain was awakened.

"**I'm sorry**"—I acknowledge the pain—mine, and sometimes another's. I admit that something went wrong.

"Please forgive me"—I take responsibility for my part: that somewhere in my memory, my beliefs, my subconscious, there is something that was activated by this. I ask for inner cleansing.

"Thank you"—I give thanks for the opportunity to heal—because this has come to the surface and can now be met consciously, instead of being carried in the dark.

"I love you"—I return to love as my foundation. Even if I can't feel it clearly right now, I declare my intention to live from love, not from hatred or resentment.

It's important to understand: Ho'oponopono is not a technique for *"quick forgiveness."* Sometimes these words need to be repeated many times—days, weeks, even months—until something in the heart begins to soften and gently let go.

How to Use Ho'oponopono in a Real Situation

Imagine this: you've been hurt—by someone's words, a betrayal, a broken promise. You feel a tight knot inside, and you admit honestly: *"I can't say 'I forgive you' right now."* And that's okay. You can begin like this.

Start with a simple, honest prayer

"Lord, You see how much this hurts. I feel wounded—angry, disappointed. I don't know how to let this go yet. But I don't want to carry it for the rest of my life. Help me walk the path of forgiveness."

Gently transition into Ho'oponopono

First, speak the words to the Divine Presence—and to yourself:

"I'm sorry. Please forgive me. Thank you. I love you."

If you can, bring the person or situation to mind

If it feels possible, picture the person or the situation in front of you—or simply hold it in your awareness—and repeat the same four phrases again, without forcing anything, at a pace that feels natural.

Sometimes, especially at first, everything inside resists: "What do you mean 'I love you'? Are you serious?"

That's normal. The goal isn't to perform holiness. The goal is to acknowledge what's true—and still, gently, keep repeating the words, like medicine that doesn't taste good at first.

Other Forms of Forgiveness Prayer

If Ho'oponopono doesn't feel close to you yet, you can use a more familiar form. For example:

"Lord, I can't forgive this person right now. There is too much pain and anger in me. But I ask You: begin this process in me. Help me, over time, to see this more broadly— to stop returning to it every minute, to stop living inside this resentment. I want to be free, but I don't know how yet. Teach me."

Or:

"Lord, I know what I'm holding inside is destroying me first. I do not justify what was done. But I don't want my life to keep being ruled by this pain. Help me, step by step, come out of this inner captivity."

A prayer like this admits honestly: *" I can't yet—but I want to learn. "* And that's enough to begin moving forward.

Forgiving Yourself

Sometimes the hardest person to forgive is not someone else—it's yourself.

For mistakes in the past. For broken relationships. For weakness, fear, and indecision. For *"not protecting," "not understanding in time," "not being there."* Here, a prayer of forgiveness can sound especially tender:

"Lord, it's hard for me to accept myself. I keep returning to the past and blaming myself for what I did—or didn't do. I see my mistakes, and I feel guilty. But if You can love me as I am, teach me to look at myself with greater kindness. I ask Your forgiveness, and I ask You to help me, little by little, forgive myself."

This is also where Ho'oponopono can be especially powerful. As you repeat the four phrases, you can gently keep your attention on yourself, as someone who makes mistakes, and is still worthy of love and healing.

Forgiveness Is a Journey

It helps to stop thinking of forgiveness as a button: press it, and everything instantly releases. More often, forgiveness is a process.

Today it feels a little lighter. Tomorrow it hits again. A week later, you remember it again. A month later, it's not as sharp. A year later, you remember—but you no longer live inside that scene.

A prayer of forgiveness is meant to accompany this journey—not to force it. You move gently, at your own pace. You can say to God:

"Lord, I'm not asking to wake up tomorrow and forget everything. I'm asking You to walk with me through this process. Help me sense when I'm ready to take the next step, and support me when it hurts again."

When Forgiveness Doesn't "Feel" Like Forgiveness

Sometimes someone says, *"I've prayed for forgiveness so many times. I've repeated these words again and again. But inside I still feel empty—or, on the contrary, hard. Does that mean I haven't forgiven? Does it mean prayer doesn't work?"*

Feelings aren't always a reliable measure. Sometimes the old reaction keeps echoing out of habit, even though your life is already changing:

- you don't return to that situation a hundred times a day;
- you don't wish harm on the person;
- you don't build your life around the pain;
- you can remember without the same intensity.

That, too, is *the* fruit of prayer—even if you don't have a clear inner feeling that says, *"I have forgiven."*

Forgiveness is not always warm. Sometimes it's a decision: *"I will no longer feed this resentment with my energy."*

The feelings may come later—or they may slowly fade on their own.

A Small Daily Practice of Forgiveness

So *that* resentment doesn't quietly accumulate over the years—and so you can live more freely and fully—you can make forgiveness part of your daily life in a very gentle way.

For example, in the evening, after your prayer of gratitude, add a few lines:

"Lord, if I hurt someone today— by a word, a tone, or indifference— forgive me, and help me see it. And if someone hurt me—consciously or not— help me not turn it into another heavy stone in my heart. I want to learn to let go more quickly, without slipping into bitterness. Teach me this."

And from time to time, return to Ho'oponopono—especially on days when you feel something old rising up inside you again.

Forgiveness is one of the deepest layers of prayer. Through it, we learn to look at ourselves and others not only with justice, but also with mercy, first of all toward ourselves. Not by justifying evil, but by refusing to keep living inside it.

In the following chapters, we'll talk about how everything we've discussed—gratitude, prayer in difficult moments, the practice of forgiveness—can come together into your personal language of prayer. And how, from that language, you can create your own prayers: simple, alive, and truly yours.

18

HOW TO CREATE YOUR OWN PRAYER: FROM FIRST WORDS TO A PERSONAL PRAYER BOOK

Many people use ready-made prayers all their lives—from prayer books, tradition, or beloved spiritual texts. There's nothing wrong with that. On the contrary, those words carry the wisdom of generations—depth that's been tested by time.

But at some point, the soul often feels a simple, natural desire: *"I want to speak to God in my own words."*

And then fear can creep in: "*What if I say something wrong?" "What if it's not 'spiritual' enough?" "What if God is 'offended' if I change the words—or simply won't hear me?"*

This chapter is an invitation to set those fears aside and try what matters most in prayer: to be real and present.

I want to help you create your own prayers—simple, honest prayers you'll actually want to return to and pray regularly. After all, prayer is a spiritual tool. And like any tool, it becomes useful through practice: if you don't use it, it gradually grows distant and unnecessary.

Why Create Your Own Prayer at All?

Ready-made prayers are like well-built roads. They're easy to walk—especially at the beginning. Your own prayer is more like a path that forms beneath your *own* steps.

It carries your lived experience. It sounds like you—your words, your tone, your personality. It makes room for your fears, hopes, and questions.

A personal prayer doesn't replace traditional texts. It adds to them. Between the canonical lines, your own living conversation with the Divine begins to appear.

And when you have at least one morning prayer, one evening prayer, and one prayer for difficult moments, you're never left without words. No matter what happens around you, the language of your own prayer will be with you.

The Main Principle: Sincerity Matters More Than Beauty

Before we talk about structure, let's name one essential thing: what matters most in prayer is not the beauty of the text, but the sincerity and intention with which you turn toward God.

God doesn't need special *"spiritual"* language. He doesn't need polished phrasing. He hears the meaning and the heart—not the style.

So when you create your own prayer, don't try to make it perfect. Let it be yours: a little uneven, repetitive in places, simple—but real.

What a Personal Prayer Can Consist Of

I'm not suggesting a rigid formula. But there are a few anchor points that can help you shape a prayer. Think of it as a gentle framework:

- an address, an honest naming of your inner state
- a request / intention / gratitude
- trust and letting go
- a short closing

Address

How do you want to speak to the Divine? *"Lord," "God," "Father," "Dear God," "Beloved Presence," "Source," "Love"*—what matters is that the word truly resonates with you.

For example:

"Lord..." "Dear God..." "Beloved Divine Presence..."

This is the first step in connection.

Honest state

Here you simply say it as it is:

"I'm afraid." "I'm confused." "I'm grateful for this day." "I'm tired, and I don't understand what's happening inside me."

No need to polish yourself. Prayer begins the moment you stop pretending.

Request / intention / gratitude

Next, name what you're bringing into the prayer:

- a request: *"Help me..."*
- an intention: *"I want to learn..."*
- gratitude: *"Thank You for..."*

Be specific:

"Help me not to snap at the people I love today."
"Show me the next step."
"Thank You for the people who are close to me."

Trust and letting go

This is the moment you acknowledge:

"I've done what I can. The rest is in Your hands."

or

"May the highest good unfold—for me and for everyone involved."

Here prayer stops being control and becomes trust.

Closing

A short phrase that gently completes the prayer:

"Amen."
"So be it."
"I trust You."

You don't have to say it out loud. But a closing helps you release the prayer inwardly—so you're not holding it with a clenched fist.

A Prayer "As You Are"

Before you try to write something *"beautiful,"* I want to suggest a simple exercise. Take a sheet of paper—or open a note on your phone. Write the date. Then write a few lines to God as if you were writing to someone you love and trust completely.

No rules. No censoring yourself. No trying to sound "right." For example:

"Lord, I don't even know where to begin. I'm tired. I'm worried about work and my mom's health. I'm angry at people who don't understand me—and at myself when I can't do what needs to be done. But I still want to feel that You are near. Help me understand what's happening in my life right now..."

That's already a prayer.

And then, if you want, you can underline a few lines—phrases that feel especially true. Over time, they can become the foundation of your personal prayer.

Three Basic Prayers: Morning, Evening, and Hard Moments

To keep from getting lost in endless variations, start with three simple anchors:

- morning
- evening
- hard moments

Your morning prayer

Ask yourself: *"What is important for me to remember in the morning? What inner state do I want to enter the day with? What do I especially need right now?"* Then shape a short prayer from your answers. For example:

"Lord, thank You for this new day. Thank You that I'm alive—that I

can breathe, feel, and move. Help me live today with less fear and more trust. Teach me to notice the good—and to bring it to others. Be with me in everything ahead. Amen."

You can shorten this prayer to two or three lines. The main thing is that the words feel like yours.

Your evening prayer

Evening prayer is about taking stock—and letting go. Ask yourself: " What mattered most today? What do I want to place in God's hands before sleep? What do I ask for as I enter the night?" For example:

"Lord, thank You for this day— for everything bright in it, and for the hard moments too. Forgive me for harsh words, for irritation, for the thoughts and judgments that pulled me away from peace and love. I let go of what I can no longer change, and I entrust to You what still weighs on me. Fill my night with peace and restoration. Amen."

Let this prayer be a gentle closing to your day.

A prayer for hard moments

This should be simple enough to remember even in panic. For example:

"Lord, I'm afraid. I don't know what to do, but please be with me. Help me feel supported—and take the next step."

Or even shorter:

"Lord, hold me. I put myself in Your hands."

If you prefer a traditional short phrase, you can say:

"Lord, save me and keep me."

You can repeat these words like a breath when you have no strength for anything else.

How to Know a Prayer Is "Yours"

There are a few signs.

You don't have to force yourself—you naturally remember it in the morning, in the evening, or in hard moments. It doesn't feel stale right away. You can repeat it for many days, and it still feels alive.

It also *registers* in the body: sometimes as warmth in the chest, sometimes as your shoulders relaxing, sometimes as a quiet exhale—like something inside finally loosens.

You can change the words without guilt. Your prayer lives and breathes with you.

And if you catch yourself repeating the words with no inner response, that doesn't mean something is "wrong" with you. It's simply a signal: it may be time to refresh the wording and ask:

"What do I really want to say to God right now?"

A Personal Prayer Book

It helps to have one place where you gather your prayers: a notebook, a journal, a document on your computer, or a note on your phone.

You can write down:

- your morning and evening prayers
- prayers that come in hard moments

- lines from traditional texts that especially speak to you
- short inner phrases that come spontaneously

Over time, this becomes your personal prayer book—not just a collection of texts, but a record of your relationship with the Divine Presence: how your questions, fears, gratitude, and requests change.

You can return to it, reread it, and notice how you are growing—and how your words become deeper, simpler, and freer.

Let Your Prayer Change with You

Remember: your prayer isn't a statue. It's a living thing. What helped you deeply a year ago may feel too narrow—or too formal—today. That's normal.

Don't be afraid to remove lines that no longer resonate. Add words that reflect the season you're in. Write new prayers—and let older ones rest.

God isn't grading your prayer like a document with tracked changes. What matters more is this: that you remain in dialogue.

Start Small

You don't need to write the *"perfect"* prayer for every situation right now. One step is enough. For example:

- Tonight: write a few honest lines to God *"as you are."*
- Tomorrow: choose two or three phrases that resonate most.
- This week: read them in the morning or evening and simply notice how you feel.

And if, over time, you create one morning prayer, one evening prayer, and one prayer for hard moments—that's already a huge step. Enough to say: *"I have my own voice in prayer. I speak to God not only with someone else's words, but with my own."*

And maybe it's through these simple, imperfect, but living words that your personal—and intimate—conversation with the Divine Presence begins... a conversation that won't end with this book.

CONCLUSION

PRAYER AS DIALOGUE: MAKING SPACE FOR AN ANSWER

Prayer is not a monologue into the void. It is a conscious encounter—a search for answers to what aches inside you, a reaching toward the Divine Presence.

Yet the answer does not always come in words. Most often, it comes as a shift in your inner state: the tightness releases, quiet clarity appears, and a simple understanding is born: I know what my first step is.

Sometimes the answer is not *"yes"* or *"no,"* but peace in the heart. Sometimes, on the contrary, it is a clear inner *"no"* that keeps you from rushing into a decision.

That's why prayer is not only about asking. It is also about making space for an answer.

After you pray, give yourself a short pause—a minute of silence without your phone or distractions. Sit a little straighter, feel your breath, and gently ask: *"What is stirring within me right now?"*

Often, what matters most is born in that minute—not a thought, but a direction.

How Answers May Come

Answers can come in different ways:

- through texts: a single line suddenly *"lights up"* and becomes personal;
- through people: the same thought unexpectedly comes through different voices;
- through events: one door closes—and soon another opens, more aligned with what you truly need;
- through the body: the right decision often brings a sense of openness and warmth;
- the wrong one, contraction;
- through conscience: a quiet inner voice that doesn't pressure you—yet doesn't let go.

It can help to remember what I call the rule of three resonances. If a direction is confirmed by your inner sense, external circumstances, and a trusted word—Scripture, a prayer text, a wise mentor—the likelihood that you are truly being guided is much higher. If only one of the three is present, give it time. Wait, watch, and let it ripen.

Another reliable measure is the fruit—what this *"answer"* produces in you. A true answer neither inflates pride nor diminishes others. It leads to simplicity, responsibility, and gratitude. Sometimes it is uncomfortable and asks for honest, difficult steps—but inside, you become freer. If what you call an "answer" demands urgent proof of your rightness, humiliation of someone else, or revenge, then it is not an answer at all, but an old wound wearing new clothes.

Silence Is Not Always Absence

Do not confuse silence with the absence of an answer. Sometimes silence is an invitation to wait. Sometimes it is an invitation to do what has long been clear—even if it is only a small step.

And sometimes God does not speak in words, but through time and signs: tomorrow you will see what you cannot see today.

A Simple Way to Deepen the Dialogue

To deepen this dialogue, it can help to keep a short prayer journal:

- date request (one or two sentences);
- your inner state after prayer;
- a possible next step.

When you return to these notes a week or a month later, you begin to notice patterns—where you truly heard, and where you were still speaking only to yourself. It's a simple but very honest way to see how your connection with the *Divine* is growing.

Freedom Is Part of a True Answer

And finally—freedom. A true answer always leaves room for your free *"yes."* It does not break you or rush you with an ultimatum. It calls you. That is the living dialogue: you speak, you are heard—and you are invited to walk only as far as you are ready to walk today.

Prayer is only one of the spiritual tools available to us for relating to the *Divine* and shaping our inner life. But in my view, it is one of the simplest—and at the same time, one of the most profound.

Prayer remains one of the most effective practices on the spiritual path. Accessible and simple, yet deeply transformative, it can become a reliable support—especially when we learn how to shape it and practice it consciously.

The form of prayer depends on the person, their tradition, and the situation they are living through. But whatever its outward form, a living prayer brings inner comfort, strengthens faith, and fills a person with a sense of connection, support, and peace.

Recently, as I was seeing my daughter off at the airport, I waved to her and quietly whispered, *"Lord, keep her safe."* Almost instantly, I felt the tension release. Inside, everything became lighter and calmer. Outwardly, nothing had changed: the plane was still on the runway—the same risks, the same unknown future. But my inner state had changed. I stopped clinging to the illusion of control and entrusted to *Him* what was already beyond my *reach*.

A prayer spoken at the right moment almost always has a steadying, healing effect—on the one who prays, and often on the space around them as well. It does not guarantee a cloudless life. But it helps us remain alive inside—no matter what the weather.

If, after reading this book, you feel you want not only to understand prayer but to truly weave it into your life—to make it regular, living, and personal—I invite you to continue this journey with me through an online practice.

In this short course, we'll learn step by step how to speak to God in our own words; how to create morning and evening prayers that truly support you; how to choose prayers for difficult seasons—fear, pain, uncertainty—and how to compile a personal prayer book you can return to again and again.

You can find details on the format and upcoming dates on my Practical Spirituality website or in the book's description.

And then—following the same logic we've returned to many times—take the first small step. The rest will unfold along the way.

ABOUT THE AUTHOR

Dmitriy Doronkin was born more than fifty years ago, half a world away, in the ancient city of Tashkent, Uzbekistan. His father was a geologist; his mother, a Russian language teacher. Growing up in the Soviet Union, where government propaganda suppressed any form of religion and spiritual freedom, Dmitriy's family never discussed religious or spiritual ideas. The ideology of communism was the only worldview offered, from kindergarten through college.

Everything changed after the Soviet Union collapsed in 1991. The Communist Party's dictatorship fell, Uzbekistan became an independent country, and a vast amount of religious and spiritual literature suddenly became available. Dmitriy gradually began discovering a completely new world. Curiosity and wonder — that is how he describes that first period of his spiritual life. Imagine being hungry for a long time, and suddenly a table with all kinds of food appears before you: some dishes you've never heard of, some look familiar, and you want to try everything.

In 1999, Dmitriy and his family moved to the United States, settling in the San Francisco Bay Area, where he still lives today. After learning English, he began reading the Bible and other religious and spiritual literature in the new language. His family attended Baptist churches in the East Bay, and he continued his self-education — but over time, his personal beliefs grew too expansive for any single denomination.

In the fall and winter of 2014, two experiences profoundly

shaped his spiritual path. The first came as an overwhelming feeling of love for everything and everyone — a feeling that gradually softened but never fully left. It remains with him to this day. The second came as guidance: one morning, while driving his daughter to school, a thought appeared in his mind with unusual clarity: "There is no WHY, only IS." It arrived from nowhere and seemed strange at first, but from that moment on, this phrase became a steady anchor in times of stress and uncertainty.

By 2015, Dmitriy's spiritual philosophy and personal beliefs had crystallized — and the next period of his spiritual growth began. That fall, he and his wife Elena were introduced to the Unity spiritual movement through a mutual friend. They became members of Unity of Walnut Creek almost immediately. In February 2016, Dmitriy completed training and became a certified Unity prayer chaplain. Later that year, he was elected to the Board of Trustees, where he served two consecutive three-year terms (2016–2022). During this time, he also taught classes on prosperity and spiritual abundance.

In early 2020, Dmitriy began developing Practical Spirituality — a personal spiritual movement rooted in his own experience, study, and practice. Practical Spirituality is not affiliated with any single religion or denomination. It draws on the wisdom of multiple traditions and offers a simple, grounded approach to spiritual growth — accessible to anyone, regardless of background or belief.

Along the way, Dmitriy was ordained as a Reverend through the Universal Life Church Ministries. While he values the recognition, he is the first to say that his spiritual authority comes not from a certificate, but from years of personal practice, study, and honest searching.

From 2024 to 2026, Dmitriy wrote *Prayer: Faith, Focus, and Words*, his first book on understanding prayer and making it a living, personal practice. The book has been published in both Russian and English.

Through Practical Spirituality, Dmitriy offers online courses on prayer and spiritual practice, as well as personal spiritual consultations for those seeking guidance on their individual path. His work is dedicated to helping people build a living, personal connection with the Divine — not through dogma, but through honest practice.

Dmitriy lives in the East Bay, California, with his wife Elena and their two corgis, Duchess and Tulip.

Learn more at **www.practicalspirituality.co**

www.ingramcontent.com/pod-product-compliance
Lightning Source LLC
LaVergne TN
LVHW010927110826
845149LV00013B/2503

* 9 7 9 8 9 9 5 8 0 9 7 1 5 *